I Just Got a Puppy.

What Do I Do?

Mordecai Siegal

AND

Matthew Margolis

Photographs by Mordecai Siegal
and Tara Darling

A FIRESIDE BOOK
Published by Simon & Schuster
New York London Toronto Sydney

FIRESIDE
Rockefeller Center
1230 Avenue of the Americas
New York, NY 10020

FIRESIDE and colophon are registered trademarks
of Simon & Schuster, Inc.

Designed by Christine Weathersbee

Manufactured in the United States of America

10   9   8   7   6

Library of Congress Cataloging-in-Publication Data

Siegal, Mordecai.
      I just got a puppy : What do I do? / Mordecai Siegal and Matthew
   Margolis ; photographs by Mordecai Siegal and Tara Darling.
         p.   cm.
      "A Fireside book."
      1. Puppies.   2. Dogs.   I. Margolis, Matthew.   II. Title.
   SF427 .S592 2002
   636.7'07—dc21   2002018868

ISBN 0-684-85520-8

For information regarding special discounts for bulk purchases,
please contact Simon & Schuster Special Sales at 1-800-456-6798 or
business@simonandschuster.com

To Mel Berger of the William Morris Agency, who just happens to be the best literary agent in the business, with gratitude and respect. Thank God he's on our side.

Acknowledgments

You've got to love a puppy. And you've got to love those who are responsible for bringing the healthy, happy ones into the world to spread their joy and pleasure. The authors would like to express their appreciation to all the people who do the right thing for puppies and those who love them.

Many, many thanks to Bill Scolnik and Rick Tomita for helping us find so many wonderful puppies (and the people they own) to photograph. They are the geniuses behind J-B Wholesale Pet Supplies Catalog and the award-winning Jacquet Kennels, which produces the finest Boxers and Shiba Inus anywhere. Their young Boxer, Timer, appears among the photos. Because of the space limitations, many photos that were taken could not be reproduced in the book as they so richly deserved. We are grateful to the following people for allowing Mordecai to photograph their beloved pups: Ruth Grimaldi; Gay Payne; Naomi David; Ryan O'Neill and Rufus (white Great Pyrenees); Irene Brydzienski and her Australian Shepherd; Susan and Gordon Levine and their three white Bichons Frisés (Patches, Shayna, and Goober); Karen Urban and her Siberian Husky, Darius; Donna, Ken, and their son, Brian Jannucci, and their Shar Pei, Midnight; Alida Comtois and her Leonberger, Esia Von Klingelberg; Lorrie Getter-Howe and her Pug; Catherine Lord and her Standard Schnauzers, Tasi and Mandy, and her Sheltie, Lea; Paul and Anita Ott and their two German Shepherds, Clarence and Cassie; Rod Beckstead and his Tibetan Spaniel; and to Rich and Linda Berberich and their four delightful Rottweiler puppies, who romped all over their young son James. A very special thank-you to rare-breed judge J. C. Harrison, whose fine writing appears in *Kennel Review* and "Dogwatch."

The training photos that appear in Chapter Nine were taken by superb Los Angeles–based photographer Bror Lawrence. His expertise and participation make an important contribution to this book.

We wish to acknowledge the generous help and patience of the dogs that appeared in the training photos and their adoptive parents. Appearing in SIT, COME, and LEASH BREAKING is Savannah, a Golden Retriever owned by Tom King. In SIT-STAY is Patty III, an Airdale owned by Walter E. and Ruth Smith. Benji, a Puli, owned by Bob and Jill Benson, is featured in DOWN (Paws Technique). Willi, a Rhodesian Ridgeback, owned by Cary Kaplan, is featured in DOWN (Hand Technique).

Contents

CONTENTS

Introduction

Puppies are full of mischief and piddle. They are fidgety, stubborn, unruly, nosy, noisy, chewy, yappy, and totally dedicated to their "incoming" and "outgoing" stuff. They drive many dog owners crazy. Their human caretakers seldom understand a dog's nature or know how to manage a dog, especially a very young one. The canine problems mount, and the puppy simply compounds things because his owners don't know what to do. But take heart. Inside every unmanageable puppy is an endearing dog waiting to bounce into his grown-up dog suit and become a normal member of your family.

Living with a huggable pup that sits quietly with his tongue hanging out is a fantasy. Even in this age of megabytes and car phones we still daydream about a puppy that will chase a tennis ball and grow up to carry the newspaper home in his mouth.

Getting a puppy is part of the American dream. But some puppies turn daydreams into nightmares. The innocent little dog curled up in his soft nest may disturb your deepest sleep by howling all night, tax your patience by peeing all over your carpet and chewing up your favorite clothes, while not coming close to being your best friend. The truth is few puppies can make your dreams come true. It's not their problem. It's yours. Reality, however, is not bad. A real puppy *will* swing his tail with pleasure when you walk through the door and *will* be honestly glad to see you. A real puppy grows up to be a real dog and can reward you with companionship and loyalty and something that's a lot like love.

There is, however, yet another puppy trap, and you are advised not to fall into it by turning the unmanaged puppy into the overmanaged puppy. We call this the Superdog or Superpuppy Syndrome. It is normal to want to make your little dog a phi beta puppy. As there are overly ambitious parents, there are also overly ambitious dog owners. The burden of great expectations is placed on the small shoulders of dogs as young as three months. There is no question that their owners have only the best intentions. But overzealous puppy parents can do more harm than good.

There have been many feature news stories on television about the trend to create "superbabies." They show infants and toddlers (still trying to get oatmeal on a spoon) being taught how to read and being exposed to great art, poetry, mathematics, and various aspects of science. The glaze in the children's eyes and their smirking faces seem to indicate that they would prefer to have their diapers changed and be allowed to run off and play. Many educators feel that some of these "superbabies" will develop learning disabilities later in childhood because the parents are circumventing the normal growth and development process. When it comes to puppies it is all too easy to create serious behavior problems by introducing intense training methods plus caveman discipline, then expecting too much, too soon.

One of the myths of dog ownership is that you should *never spoil your puppy*. This is simply incorrect. It is a popular misconception that puppies must behave themselves at all times and that you must constantly discipline them and never let them get away with anything. In the beginning, expect puppies to do most things wrong. It is our responsibility to educate ourselves so that the *appropriate* methods are used to teach as we nurture a little dog.

For most dogs, maturity is reached at the end of the first year of life, although giant breeds mature a little later. Typically, puppies are taken to their new homes between two and three months of age. Try to compare a three- to five-month-old puppy to a nursery school or kindergarten child; a five- to seven-month-old dog to a grade schooler; a seven- to twelve-month-old dog to a teenager.

How much can you expect from a child in nursery school or kindergarten? Do not misunderstand: This is an important time for puppies as well as children. Rules must be established, but they should be more like boundary posts at first. Puppies must negotiate a learning process before we can expect them to behave like obedient angels. The learning process must not be harsh or unforgiving. A firm, demanding approach to training comes later, and even then it depends on the dog's temperament. The most important first step to managing your puppy properly is to develop a warm relationship with the dog, which is known as *bonding*. Gentle teaching comes next. Your puppy deserves good marks just for being himself. What we're looking for is your *rapport card,* with A's in Patience, Kindness, and Understanding. You just got a puppy. What do you do? Read on, dear dog owner, read on.

ONE

YOUR PUPPY'S BEGINNINGS

Your puppy's former life, no matter how brief, has a lasting influence on his behavior. All puppies, of course, present us with some annoying behavior that is part of their growth and development. It is similar to raising children. But there are some puppy problems that can challenge you beyond your natural limits, especially if this is your first dog. For example, all puppies will try to nip your fingers when they are teething or experiencing a random aggressive urge. But what do you do with one that nips all the time? His teeth could hurt you, and if this problem is not dealt with properly, the dog could grow up to become a serious biter. The same is true of a puppy that constantly yaps and yipes. He will become an excessive barker once his voice changes. And then there are those puppies that seem frightened of everything, even you. They cringe with fear at the least disturbance, such as the ringing of the doorbell or an unfamiliar person entering your house. Your puppy's behavior reflects his identity or personality. What happened (or what didn't happen) to the little dog before you got him helped to create much of his behavior.

A dog's behavior is the result of a combination of factors. It is partly inherited from his parents, grandparents, and other relatives. It is also learned from the dog's mother and littermates. But it can be dramatically influenced for good or bad by human handling and external events in the dog's life.

A dog that inherits a gentle, even temperament and is taught the social rules of a dog pack by his mother may still become a difficult animal if he was abused by humans or continually frightened by a threatening environment. The impact of abusive treatment or negative living conditions can alter or distort a normal dog's behavior. For this reason it is important for new dog owners to know something about their puppy's former living conditions.

Understanding the source of your puppy will increase your sensitivity to him and help you develop patience with his shortcomings as well as increase your ability to deal with some of the dog's problem behavior more effectively.

Do not misunderstand: We are not suggesting that you can actually change a dog's temperament or even his inclinations. However, you can learn to control your dog's behavior to make life more pleasant for both of you. A puppy with an aggressive temperament may always be an aggressive dog. However, once he has been brought under your control he may be manageable so that he will not unleash his aggressive behavior and become dangerous. Similarly, a shy puppy will probably grow into a shy dog, but that does not necessarily mean he has to live in total fear of every new person, place, or thing.

Many of you who already have a puppy may never know much about his past life. We will attempt to describe what your puppy *may* have experienced if he was purchased from a breeder's kennel, a pet shop, a shelter, or a private individual. Many sound dogs have come from every conceivable source. Many not-so-sound dogs have also come from every conceivable source. The following descriptions of puppy sources are meant to help people understand the *possible* reasons for their puppy's behavior. They are not meant as a guide for buying puppies. It would be meaningless to prejudge any source of puppies without an on-site evaluation.

Noncommercial Breeders

Noncommercial breeders establish kennels (usually in their homes) for the purpose of creating purebred puppies through carefully selected matings. They are expected to be knowledgeable, skillful, and humane in their methods. They are responsible for producing almost all the dogs that compete in the show ring and other areas of the dog sport such as field trials. Dogs that compete for prizes such as Best-in-Show ribbons, and for titles such as Champion, are the "show-and-tell" of noncommercial breeders. Such dogs must be conceived, whelped, and raised in the best possible circumstances if their breeders hope to succeed with them and establish important reputations.

Of course, the hit-or-miss element is always present when breeding dogs, even when the breeder understands genetics, pedigrees, and selective mating. What results is an abundance of puppies that do not meet the standard of perfection of their breed and cannot hope to compete successfully as show dogs or field dogs. The coat color or length may be off just a bit, or one paw may turn outward too much. The slightest flaw may disqualify a puppy as a competitor. Only a few puppies are ever considered "show quality." No matter how beautiful, how delightful, or how perfect in every other way, they are sold as "pet quality" dogs. These puppies usually have the most going for them as healthy, happy dogs and often make truly wonderful pets.

The best of the kennels breed their bitches only once a year, if that often. Before allowing mating to occur, conscientious breeders have their dogs examined and X-rayed to avoid passing on serious medical conditions to future generations. With few exceptions, puppies raised in noncommercial kennels receive outstanding care. They are inoculated against disease, fed properly, housed in clean, ample spaces free of parasites, and kept warm in the winter and cool in the summer. Most have large areas for exercise and play.

One of the most important aspects of puppies from reputable breeders is the positive result of their *socializing* techniques. The concept of socializing young puppies stems from serious research and is now the common practice of most noncommercial breeders. (For more about socializing, see Chapter Five.) They have learned that a socialized puppy will more easily and happily adapt to the human environment, and many dog trainers believe these puppies are easier to train.

Noncommercial breeders usually do not sell their puppies until they are at least eight weeks old, and many hold on to them even longer than that. Dogs that remain with their mother and littermates for at least eight weeks are healthier, happier animals and adjust better to other dogs. Most noncommercial breeders are fussy about who may purchase their puppies. They are usually quite determined that each one of their puppies goes to a good home with careful, responsible owners. They will not sell their little dogs to anyone they suspect will not provide a proper home.

One of the negatives is behavior that develops if a puppy remains in the kennel longer than twelve to sixteen weeks. Housebreaking becomes more difficult as time passes because kennel life permits urination and defecation to take place anytime, anywhere and this behavior requires more effort to change.

Many breeders house their dogs in separate, indoor-outdoor kennels rather than in their homes. This can cause a difficult behavior adjustment for young dogs when they are introduced to their new homes after spending the first part of their lives in a dog run. They may bark excessively; chew furniture, clothing, and carpets; dig up yards; behave aggressively, and get into all sorts of mischief. Young dogs leaving their kennel life behind them after four or more months may require special consideration, handling, and training.

When looking for the right puppy, selecting a breeder can be as difficult as selecting a dog from any other source. The American Kennel Club (AKC) suggests contacting a dog club in your area or the national club of the breed of your choice for breeder recommendations. AKC will provide lists of these clubs.

Upon request, and without charge, the United Kennel Club (UKC) of Kalamazoo, Michigan, refers prospective buyers to breeders on their Breeders List. The UKC has historically encouraged breeders to create dogs that not only look good in dog shows but work or hunt as well.

Commercial Breeders

There are puppy breeders in suburban and rural areas that sell their animals directly to pet owners and to local pet shops. These breeders generate litters of puppies for pet owners and are in business for one reason only: profit. They advertise in newspapers and depend on a word-of-mouth reputation. Many of them are reputable businesspeople who maintain clean, healthy kennel operations with a variety of dog breeds. Their purposes are different from those of the noncommercial breeders, who are interested in developing a champion line of purebred dogs. The commercial breeders' success is based solely on the satisfaction of their customers.

If the proprietor refuses to tell you, it is impossible to determine if puppies from this source are the result of selective breeding, if the dogs mated were screened for medical and behavior problems, if they were carefully socialized after the third week of life. However, it is possible to determine by careful observation if puppies from this source were treated humanely, if the dogs were housed adequately, fed properly, are in good physical condition, and are not unusually aggressive or shy. If your puppy came from one of these establishments, try to find out what the surroundings were like and then relate that to his temperament and behavior. It is worth calling the proprietor or paying him a visit.

Pet Shops

Hundreds of thousands of dogs are purchased each year from pet shops, and countless puppies from pet shops become endearing pets. However, many pet-shop dogs are born with, or develop, behavior problems. Some do not exhibit the typical behavior of their breed. There are several possible reasons for these problems, and they stem from how the animals were reared as newborns.

Some pet shops breed their own dogs and some purchase their puppies from breeders in their immediate area. Such stores are likely to offer good dogs, with only an occasional, minimal problem. However, many pet shops, particularly chain-store operations, have no control over the quality of the puppies they sell. They must rely on a system of mass-produced puppies that are sold on a wholesale basis. Most of these retail shops purchase their puppies from "livestock" brokers. These brokers either produce the animals themselves or purchase them in large quantities from many small farms and breeding operations in rural areas of the country. These are the so-called puppy mills, and they and their brokers are found mostly in the midwestern United States (Kansas, Missouri, Illinois, Nebraska, Iowa, and Minnesota, among several others). Humane societies, the media, dog trainers, and various animal professionals are highly critical of puppy-mill breeders and the unfortunate dogs they produce. They consider puppy mills to be inhumane breeding establishments that mate dogs indiscriminately, without regard for inherited medical or temperament problems, and that mate dogs too young, too old, or too frequently. Puppy mills mass-produce puppies in unsanitary, unhealthy, and cruel living conditions; dogs may freeze in winter and smolder in the summer. These unfortunates are often traumatized as well during shipment from kennel to pet shop.

When a litter of puppies is not the result of a carefully selected mating, documented by meticulous record keeping and pedigree inspection, its genetic background is a mystery. It becomes a crapshoot whether the puppies will inherit a major medical problem, such as hip displasia, heart disease, eye disorders, skin rashes, neurological disorders, or many other serious conditions. Also unknown are the inherited behavioral tendencies. When very shy or very aggressive dogs are mated, the chances are high of producing puppies of the same temperament. When dogs are constantly and indiscriminately mated, they are genetic timebombs with unpredictable possibilities. Of course, these same possibilities exist in puppies acquired from *some* noncommercial breeders as well. But a breeder's reputation precedes him or her, and a careful shopper has a better chance of getting a quality dog from such a source.

Mass-produced puppies are never socialized, that is, tenderly held every day during the critical period of their infancy, which would make them more adaptive to humans and other dogs. They are rarely, if ever, protected from abuse from other dogs. They are frequently born and raised in an uncaring, stressful environment and, at times, physically abused. Mass-produced puppies are often raised in unsanitary conditions, housed in cramped cages with painful mesh-wire flooring, poorly fed, and given precious little medical care. Such puppies are often psychologically damaged as well by the stress of being removed prematurely from their mothers and littermates, usually within one month of birth.

It is difficult, if not impossible, to calculate the harmful effects from the trauma created by these events. Emotional stress in a dog creates physical reactions that make profound demands on his body. The dog's body activity increases dramatically during periods of stress, making great demands on all its internal systems. This can result in increased susceptibility to illness and can create behavioral problems.

Once in the pet shops, the puppies *may* find themselves in clean, healthy surroundings, where they are well fed, given veterinary attention, and handled with sensitivity . . . or they may not. If they are displayed in a window with many other puppies, they will certainly be vulnerable to other medical problems. If a puppy is bullied by the others, it may become aggressive or shy.

It is important for the owners of pet-shop dogs to understand what their pets probably experienced before they reached the comfort and stability of their new homes. Pet-shop puppies may require more patience and tender loving care than usual. If there are any signs of extreme behavior, the dog should be evaluated by a professional dog trainer.

Animal Shelters

Getting a dog from a shelter is a life-saving gesture that is both good for the dog and for you. Some shelters are run by animal-control agencies or local governments whose mission is to reduce the stray dog and cat population. Because of limited time, space, and budget, these agencies must destroy the animals that are not claimed or adopted within a short period of time. When you adopt an animal, you are literally saving its life.

There are thousands of government and nongovernment animal welfare organizations throughout North America and they can be found in the Yellow Pages under "Animal Shelters." These are often the safest, most efficient, economical sources for acquiring healthy dogs. A full-service organization is staffed with professionals and experts, including veterinarians, technicians, administrators, handlers, peace officers, humane-educational specialists, and even dog trainers.

An adopted dog from a shelter is likely to have been examined by a veterinarian and treated if necessary with vaccinations and surgical neutering. Despite medical screening, there can be no certainty that the dog has not inherited a tendency toward some disease or medical condition. Other than the dog's apparent behavior, there is usually no prior knowledge of the animal's temperament or its causes. Many dogs in shelters have simply been given up or abandoned because the former owners could not afford to keep them or no longer had the desire. Some dogs end up in shelters because their owners cannot cope with the very behavior problems they unintentionally created themselves.

Although some shelters are better than others, life for a dog in a shelter is not happy. The dogs are confined in small, indoor runs with many other dogs, and there is little or no personal attention. A lost or abandoned dog in such circumstances is likely to be in a state of emotional stress. There is the constant barking and howling of fear, anxiety, and confusion. Dogs lucky enough to be removed from this environment and placed in a home *must* be allowed a period of adjustment to calm down and settle in.

Private Sources

You may have acquired your puppy from a friend or neighbor, or you may have responded to a notice on the wall of a veterinarian's office. Either way, it is important to get as much information about the puppy's previous life as possible. Knowledge of the puppy's parents is helpful, but what you really need is the puppy's behavioral and medical history.

Was the puppy fed properly, treated kindly, given loving attention every day, medically examined, vaccinated, allowed to play, not bullied by other puppies or grown dogs, given a comfortable environment to live in, free of stress? The answers to these questions will explain much about the little dog's current behavior and potential problems. With loving kindness, patience, and sensible dog training, you and your puppy will be able to deal with most problems caused by poor breeding and early puppy experiences.

T W O

BONDING WITH YOUR PUPPY

Is there any member of the family more consistent, more reliable, trustworthy, giving, or loving than your dog? Probably not. However, as magical as the family dog is, he doesn't get that way by magic. If you've had any experience with dogs at all, then you know it doesn't always work out between every dog and every family. And even though it's terribly upsetting for the humans involved, it's far worse for the dog. In some cases, it can actually be fatal.

When you live with a new dog there is one thing that must come before training commands or even housebreaking: the creation of a bond between the dog and one or more members of the household. This is the development of an emotional tie between the family pet and everyone living with him. A new dog, young or old, must feel that he belongs, that he is a part of the family. Once the dog has been exposed to human contact during the earliest phase of puppyhood, his desire to become part of the human family is strong.

The Family Dog

So how do you create a good family dog? In order to explain that, we must first establish what exactly is a family. People, like dogs, are family creatures. But not all families consist of mothers, fathers, children, and grandparents. Many are quite untraditional; they consist of various types of people spending some part of their lives together.

People band together out of common interests, a need for other people, for companionship, for intimacy, and for a bit of comfort, warmth, and security. As John Lennon wrote, "I get by with a little help from my friends." Make no mistake about it, all of us need our families, no matter what kind they are, just as dogs do. Dogs band together because they are pack animals and live in groups that share the responsibilities for survival. A dog fits into the human family quite well but relates to it as a substitute dog pack.

The traditional human family consists of a mother, a father, and one or more children. But a family can also be a mother and a daughter. A nephew and an aunt. Two friends, two lovers, *or one person and a dog. If you* don't mind, the dog certainly won't.

You could define a family as simply two or more creatures sharing their lives. For better or for worse, that is the essence of family life. And a dog will always fit into the equation, if you give it the opportunity.

If you already have a family, then why do you need a dog? Possibly for protection, companionship, or for the fun of it. But whatever the reason, a dog adds one more presence in your life for you to love and to love you back. It's why we have babies. But is having a dog anything like having a baby? In some ways it is and in others there is no similarity at all.

The Four-Legged Baby

Both babies and puppies are helpless and totally dependent, and both need to be protected from themselves. So we baby-proof a house and we puppy-proof a house. Both are adorable, huggable, lovable, enchanting, enticing, playful, demanding, noisy, irritating, and manage to keep us up much of the night.

So what are the differences between a puppy and a baby? A puppy will never grow up and go off to college, forget to write home, and then show up unannounced with six friends for dinner and a load of dirty laundry. Of course, a child will throw a graduation cap into the air someday, look his or her parents in their teary eyes and say, "Thanks folks, for everything you've done for me." A puppy can't do that. But a puppy *can* grow into an adult dog and love you, adore you, and stay with you till the end.

The principal difference between children and puppies is their view of the world. Children grow up and go out into the world on their own. Puppies grow up, stay home, and try to live in harmony with you. That is the clue for making your dog a happy member of the family. It involves the element of harmony, and it is so easy to accomplish.

Three Requirements for Succeeding with Your Puppy

So how do you get a new dog to enter family life with ease and comfort and create harmony? There are three important aspects to this. The first, and probably the most important, is bonding with your dog. The second is understanding your dog. And the third is learning to control your dog. That's all there is to it.

This chapter deals with the concept of *bonding* between pet owners and their dogs. Bonding techniques are no longer considered a new concept in child raising. It is a new idea, however, for humans and their pets. When humans bond with each other they develop strong feelings that create long-term relationships. This is not quite the same as *pair-bonding* between dogs, wolves, or coyotes. When they pair-bond it is for the purpose of mating and rearing pups.

When you successfully create a bond with your puppy, everything falls neatly into place. Obedience training becomes easier, behavior problems are fewer and less intense, and your ability to enjoy your dog is greatly enhanced.

When you establish a bond with your dog, you give him a sense of security. It tells him he is loved as a member of the family and helps him adjust more easily to his new home. He'll be able to cope with anything providing he is with those who love him. Bonding with your dog makes all good things possible between you. Although it is not difficult to create a bond with a dog, it is best accomplished with a few easy techniques and an awareness of what is happening.

It is important to understand that behavior patterns in dogs develop early. What happens to a young dog in a new home in the first few weeks has a profound influence on his behavior for the rest of his life. By five weeks of age, puppies tend to imitate those who are around them the most: their mothers and littermates. It is the beginning of behavior that is learned rather than behavior that is instinctive. But puppies are also influenced positively or negatively by human attitudes, handling, and behavior toward them. The manner in which a human relates to his or her dog helps determine the dog's behavior patterns and may play a role in shaping the animal's temperament. It definitely shapes the nature of the relationship between the dog and the family it lives with.

Bonding with your dog creates feelings of love, pleasure, and a desire to nurture and protect him. To bond with your dog is to learn how to love him. Dogs that are bonded with their families usually have a strong desire to please them. Bonding with your dog also paves the way for easier training, because the dog trusts you.

There is no way to know what your new dog has experienced before he came to live with you. He may have been socialized with both other dogs and humans by a knowledgeable breeder, and treated well, or his previous life may have been a nightmare.

Whether you are dealing with a dog from a bad source, such as a puppy mill, or from a proper breeder or a shelter, you have an opportunity to communicate to your new dog that he is safe, cherished, and loved. This can also apply to a dog that has been living with you for a while. It *is* possible to change the existing relationship with your dog for the better.

How to Bond with Your Dog

Given that this is a book written by dog trainers, you may be surprised at the next statement: *The first thing to do with a new puppy is to communicate your affection and not worry so much about dog training.*

Because new puppies have no inhibitions, training, or physical control, they are going to soil the floor whenever they need to and wherever they happen to be. That means you must begin some form of housebreaking or paper training *immediately.* But we urge you to be as gentle as possible and avoid harsh discipline when doing this. Your puppy needs to get comfortable in his new home, and strict training from the first day interferes with the creation of a bond between you. Let him sniff around, learn where everything is, and get to know you before getting down to business.

Remember, the idea that you must *never spoil your puppy* is a misconception. Although puppies must be controlled, it is a mistake to constantly discipline them and never let them get away with anything. Expect puppies to do most things wrong in the beginning. Do not be harsh with your puppy. Think of yourself more as a teacher than a disciplinarian. Emotional nurturing is the key to creating a bond with your little dog. In the beginning, getting everyone in the family to relate to the new dog in a happy, loving way, with hugging, touching, and talking, is far more important than discipline.

Happy Talk

Talking to your puppy is an essential ingredient for bonding. You may feel goofy talking to your dog, but you will be helping the process. No one ever went wrong having a long talk with a dog. Your tone of voice conveys all a dog needs to know about how you feel about him.

The same is true when talking to a newborn baby. We tend to get sappy as we hold the infant in the air and giggle and gurgle aloud. Most babies enjoy the attention you're giving them, even if you're making a fool of yourself. It must be true, because they either smile or listen very seriously. Everyone is interesting to a new baby, and everything you do or say has an influence.

Puppies respond to the human voice in much the same way. They listen attentively when you talk to them, but unlike babies, they do not look you in the eyes. This is an intricate part of dog behavior having to do with dominance and subordination as an aspect of pack behavior (see Chapter Five). Do not use harsh, loud, angry tones with your puppy, especially if you want to create a bond. When you speak with a soft tone of voice, you soothe and calm your puppy. If you use a high-pitched falsetto sound with enthusiasm, the puppy will become happily curious, energized, and will respond with pleasure like a baby being tickled under the chin. Whether your voice is soothing or playful, it creates an emotional tie between you and your dog that promotes love and trust. Your voice is almost as important to the bonding process as your hands. When you speak sweet nothings to your puppy, you have at your disposal an important tool for shaping a relationship with your dog that will last for the rest of his life.

Use a very high, falsetto tone of voice with extravagance and abandon. It is extraordinary how effective this is for getting a dog's trust, interest, and enthusiasm. It works miracles. Most dogs will slip instantly into a happy frame of mind and will be willing to do anything in the world for you. Imagine getting on your knees in front of a puppy and squeaking out in a falsetto voice, "Hello, Captain Dog, how are you? Are you ready to work for me today? Oh, yes, yes! What a good dog!" It's hilarious, but it works.

A variation of this is to sing to your dog. Not only will you help the bonding process, but you will be an important source of entertainment for the dog . . . and the rest of your family. Lift your head up high and howl out your song. If wolves can do it, so can you.

Hold Me, Touch Me

Go ahead, touch it. Your puppy's belly cries out to to be rubbed and petted. With few exceptions, all puppies want to be held, rubbed, stroked, petted, scratched, squeezed, and gently pulled. You only have to watch a litter of puppies together to see what happens naturally. The mother licks them, shoves them, picks them up with her teeth and moves them around. At feeding time the puppies huddle together and muddle into each other to get a fair share of milk. When they nap they pile up and sleep like one mound of fur. When they play they are constantly pawing at each other and rolling around, one on top of the other. A dog is a sensual creature and lives mostly by what he can see, hear, touch, and smell. Dogs cannot intellectualize about their feelings. Your dog craves physical contact with you. It is an important expression of your love and good feeling about him. It is always a pleasant surprise to the novice dog owner when her pet walks up to her and places his head under her hand, asking to be petted. It is an endearing gesture. *Hold me, touch me* is a major part of the bonding process. Be extravagant with your physical expressions of endearment with your puppy. Nothing establishes the bond quicker.

Environmental Protection

Another aspect of bonding involves teaching your puppy about the house he lives in and his place in it. This also includes establishing the dog's daily routines. Each time you play with your puppy take him from room to room so that he can see each one, smell it, and understand where it is. This will give the dog a perspective on the boundaries of his territory so that he can maintain the small part of it that is his. Establish one place for the dog to sleep and do not change it. Place his possessions there, including toys, bedding, rawhide chews, whatever. Next, decide where you want his feeding place, resting place, play area to be, and establish boundaries for him—where he is allowed to go and where he is not allowed to go. It is important to accomplish this in a casual, happy manner so that there are no negative associations with his home. Having his own territory will ultimately be satisfying and will offer him one more reassurance about his place in the family.

Playing Around

When you're bonding with your dog it is important to teach without punishments or harsh corrections. Play with your dog whenever you can, providing it does not interfere with the puppy's need for food and rest. Give him several periods of exercise, involving tossed toys and rolled balls and ending with small food treats.

How you play with your dog is important. It must be done in a *positive* manner. Get down on the floor and make yourself available. Play with him, roll over with him, and do the sort of things you would with a crawling baby. Allow your play to involve cuddling and hugging. Avoid games that encourage aggressive behavior. Do not "box" with your puppy or encourage him to pull with his teeth. Forget tug-of-war and I've-got-your-nose. Do not create a relationship based on bitten fingers and slaps on the face. What is cute at three months of age can be ugly and dangerous in an adult dog. Remember, if the dog misbehaves, do *not* hit him. You wouldn't do that to a baby, and you shouldn't do it to a puppy.

In a Family Way

It is impossible for everyone to relate to the family dog in the same way. And vice versa. That's to be expected. What is important is that everyone accept the new dog as a member of the family and find a way to establish some sort of a relationship with him. Anyone living in the house should make an effort to bond with the new dog on some meaningful level.

There is usually one person who ends up providing most of the dog's needs, but it is best if those responsibilities are divided up. For example, the person who is the first one up should take the puppy out for his morning walk, and someone else can give him his first meal of the day, and so on. It is surprising to learn how fast a bond can be established when someone does just one thing for the dog on a daily basis.

When the puppy first arrives, everyone in the household makes a great fuss over him. But once he's been there for a while the excitement dies down and everyone is faced with the reality and responsibility of living with a new dog. While some members of the family will continue to be enthusiastic about the dog, others may not. That is understandable. But if the household is to have a nice experience with the new dog, everyone must make an effort to establish some kind of a bond. A person doesn't have to go ga-ga every time they see the dog. But talking to him, touching him, and doing one small thing for him each day will go very far in establishing an important tie with the animal.

Some children think of their pets as younger siblings. It is best not to interfere with that, unless the dog is in danger of being abused. Usually, when a child considers a new puppy in the house to be like a brother or sister it is a good situation. Some children regard their pet as a new, close friend, while some parents think of the puppy as another child. It really doesn't matter what the relationship means to each member of the family, just as long as the dog is treated well. The wonderful thing about a dog is that he will accept any kind of relationship you want provided it is based on kindness and love.

Bonding Activities

Here are some activities that help create a strong bond between dogs and their families:

Give your dog a friendly name and then use it frequently. This is not only good for the dog but keeps you in a pleasant frame of mind when you deal with him. If you name your dog Stupid or Barfy, something unpleasant will be reflected in your manner. There is simply no way to call a dog Stupid in a nice way.

Feed your dog with affection, walk your dog with pleasure and excitement, bathe him in a soothing manner, and comb and brush him gently. Take him with you frequently on errands and while shopping, allow the dog to be with you while doing chores, and exercise him in a playful manner. There are other bonding activities that are sure to win his heart and make you smile, too.

Bonding with your dog does not take a very long time. For some it can happen in fifteen minutes. For others it may take anywhere from one day to one week. It may happen quickly, but it lasts for a lifetime.

THREE

Unraveling the Mystery of Your Puppy's Personality

The Five Most Important Tests
Your Dog Will Ever Take

If you already have your puppy, it's urgent that you find out who he is and what he is like so you can determine what kind of a dog he will most likely become. Most people go about getting a puppy as though they were on a TV game show. "Should I choose door number one, or take what's behind the curtain?" Few people would make a guessing game out of buying a house or a car, but that is often what happens when they purchase a creature that is going to live with them for fifteen years and influence their lives in a major way. Few people know how to go about selecting a puppy correctly unless they've been taught how. Especially if you are not able to understand your puppy's pedigree (assuming he has one), are not able to examine his parents for temperament, or are unsure of the source of the dog, it is of great importance to understand his personality so that you can deal with him successfully and avoid as many problems as possible.

Puppies are fun. They climb, they tumble, and they lick everything in sight, including your toes and your ears. But it's difficult to predict how they will behave as grown dogs unless you understand something about their temperaments from the start. Even young puppies have specific personalities, or temperaments, and handling them should be based on their individual traits if you want them to develop into enjoyable dogs. Every puppy is a surprise package with a specific kind of dog waiting to hop out once it's unwrapped. The five tests in this chapter will unwrap the package and solve the mystery of your puppy's real personality. This will take the guesswork out of handling the dog properly. The results of these tests will enable you to understand what kind of a dog you really have and adapt your approach to his needs. When you know what you're doing, you can make your dog's everyday experiences—with you and everyone else—pleasant and as problem-free as possible. Please note that when we use the terms *temperament* and *personality,* we mean the same thing.

These tests will also be useful in solving behavioral and social problems that all puppies have, such as pulling you down the street, piddling on the floor, or begging for food at the table. A dog's ability to learn is affected by his personality, which in turn should influence how you train your dog or solve his behavior problems. Dog training is based on the proper application of instructions, praise, and corrections. *How* to apply these techniques should be determined by the dog's personality. This is an important point.

For example, if your puppy has a shy personality and you scold him severely for housebreaking accidents, you may do more harm than good. Harsh treatment may stop a shy dog from soiling in the kitchen, but it could cause him to uncontrollably wet the floor everywhere else whenever he sees you. This could also prevent him from ever developing a happy, loving relationship with humans. We often create new problems by the way we solve an existing one. Do not win the battle and lose the war. Understanding your puppy's personality makes all the difference.

About the Tests

These tests can be given to any dog seven weeks or older and are easy to do. But do not be deceived by their simplicity. The results will be sure to enlighten you. Each test begins with an introduction that gives essential information, including the purpose of the test. This is followed by How to Give the Test, which is an easy-to-understand set of instructions. The third part, Test Results, is divided into two matching columns, Reaction and Personality. The various sets of reactions will match up with one of the six personality types as they pertain to your dog. The six personality types are: (1) Responsive, (2) High Energy, (3) Strong Willed, (4) Shy/Insecure/Timid, (5) Calm/Easygoing, and (6) Aggressive. The Aggressive personality is divided into

Aggressive (Dominant) and Aggressive (Fear); they are dealt with separately.

Many of you will discover that your puppy has different personality reactions in two or more of the tests. This is normal. Even a puppy can be complex. If that happens, use your common sense to determine your puppy's primary personality category. For example, there can be no mistaking an aggressive personality if the dog's reactions are extremely aggressive in one or more of the tests. We urge you to take the short time involved and test your puppy. Based on the results, you can determine which one of the six personality categories best describes your puppy. Then allow that knowledge to influence how you relate to your dog, especially when training him or solving behavior problems. Following Five Personality Tests is a final section describing the Six Personality Types. Here you will learn how to use your understanding of your dog's temperament in training and everyday handling. Knowing your dog's personality type will help you create a stronger, more satisfying bond with him. It means you can avoid many potentially upsetting episodes by simply avoiding situations he cannot handle well. By knowing your dog you will be better equipped to bring out the best in him and cope with his limitations. Because bonding with your dog and developing a sound relationship is very important, these tests are invaluable. You and your dog will benefit greatly from them.

Five Personality Tests

1. How Friendly Is Your Dog?

Social Attraction Test

The purpose of this test is to determine your dog's reaction to people. Is your dog friendly? Is he responsive to people? Is he a social animal? He may be shy or aggressive. The results of this test will help you handle your dog properly when dealing with visitors or when encountering people outside your home. For example, a Shy/Insecure/Timid dog should be exposed to as many new situations and people as possible without forcing the situation. Very often, shyness turns into aggression as the dog matures unless he is handled properly. He must be treated in an extremely friendly manner and learn that new people should not be feared. The same is true for an aggressive dog. However, if he misbehaves, he must be corrected firmly. Your dog's temperament will determine how you should relate to him. If your dog needs help in this area, you must be positive in the way you deal with him. How friendly is your dog? How friendly do you want him to be with strangers? Bear in mind that as far as your dog is concerned the world is made up mostly of strangers. These are issues for concern.

How to Give the Test

Put your puppy in a quiet area, about six feet away from you. You may stand or kneel down. Either whine like a dog or talk to your puppy affectionately until you get a reaction. Use a high-pitched tone that gets his attention. The puppy's reaction indicates whether he responds in a socially acceptable way and how he deals with his curiosity.

Test Results

Reaction	Personality
Cocks his head to one side or the other. His ears become alert. His tail wags. He has a happy expression on his face. He runs to you playfully. Gets excited. Barks and talks to you. Jumps all over you.	Responsive

Reaction	Personality
A positive response. Cocks his head to one side. Gets very excited. Does not pay attention right away because he is distracted. Jumps all over you. He barks, runs back and forth. Nips or mouths your hands. Yips a lot.	High Energy

Reaction	Personality
Looks very alert. Stands and looks at you. Stands and barks at you. Barks at you and backs away. Runs up to you. Lies down near you but not next to you. Looks challenging.	Strong Willed

Reaction	Personality
Whines back at you. Backs away. Barks at you. Looks timid but curious. Crawls to you. Tail goes down. Ears go back. Looks frightened. Submissive posture. Licks your hands and seeks your reassurance.	Shy/Insecure/ Timid

Reaction	Personality
Looks at you but does not move. Becomes alert but loses interest quickly. Comes over to you slowly. Snuggles up to you. Turns away.	Calm/Easygoing

Reaction	Personality
Lunges at you. Curls lips. Growls. Acts very bold. Ears erect. Tail goes straight up.	Aggressive (Dominant)

Reaction	Personality
Growls. Curls lips. Barks. Backs away. Aggressive behavior but adopts a defensive posture. Tail down. Crouching body position.	Aggressive (Fear)

2. How Sensitive Is Your Dog to Noises?

Sound Response Test

The purpose of this test is to determine if your puppy is noise shy, which leads to other problems. For example, some dogs chew destructively as a reaction to the fear they experience in response to certain noises. Fearful reactions to noise are sometimes responsible for making a dog shy with people or wary of various aspects of the environment. If a sudden noise occurs while you and your dog are walking down the street, he might have a severe reaction to it. He might panic, run away, or stand paralyzed with fear. This type of response can be inherited or caused by a traumatic experience, such as abuse by humans, gunfire, or thunder. He might cringe when something is dropped on the floor close to him.

If your dog is noise shy, you should *never* holler at him or scold him severely. The results of this test will influence how you should teach, correct, or relate to your dog. A noise-shy dog should be spoken to in a reassuring, reasonable manner. Noise-shy dogs are at their best when handled in a gentle, loving way. They should be exposed to as many new situations as possible where noises can be introduced in a gradual and positive manner. Being noise shy is a safety issue, a behavioral issue, and definitely a bonding issue.

How to Give the Test

You will need a shake can for this test. This is simply an empty soda can with five or ten pennies inside so that it rattles when shaken. (Refer to Chapter Four for more details.)

Place your puppy in a quiet area, about six feet away from you. The test is given in two parts. Part one requires that you shake the can vigorously behind your back. We do not want the puppy (or mature dog) to see the source of the noise; it is useful to know how your puppy will react to a source of noise he cannot see. Part two requires that you toss the can six to ten feet away from the dog. *Under no circumstances should you throw the can directly at the dog.* The dog should never be made to feel that he is being threatened. When the shake can is tossed within the dog's view, he may react differently than he did to the first part of the test, giving you another insight into his nature.

If you suspect that your puppy (or grown dog) has an aggressive personality, do not toss the can. To emphasize this point we have entered no reactions for part two of the test in the Aggressive Personality section.

Test Results

Reaction	Personality
(Can behind your back) Becomes alert to the noise with his ears erect. A curious look on his face. Tries to locate the sound. Comes up to you and looks around.	Responsive
(Can tossed) Goes to the can. Plays with it. Tries to pick it up in his mouth and bring it to you. He runs around with it in his mouth. Pounces on it.	Responsive
(Can behind your back) Becomes alert to the noise with his ears erect, but is more distracted by sights and sounds around him. He does not pay	High Energy

attention and loses interest quickly.
He barks at the noise. He jumps
on you and runs around you with
excitement, looking for the noise.
(Can tossed)   High Energy
Goes up to the can and tries
to run away with it. It becomes
a game. He tries to pounce on it
and growls at it playfully. Or he
does not pay attention to it and
becomes excited about other
things around him.

(Can behind your back)   Shy/Insecure/Timid
Hears the noise and backs away.
Lowers his ears and tail. The hair
on his neck goes up. Submissive
posture. Makes a yelping sound.
Tries to turn away. Barks at you.
(Can tossed)   Shy/Insecure/Timid
Becomes startled. Barks, cries,
runs away. Submissive body
posture. Ears and tail go down.
Hackles go up. Runs to you out
of fear or insecurity.

(Can behind your back)   Calm/Easygoing
Hears the noise and slowly walks
up to you. Looks up and then
goes back to what he was doing.
Is either totally uninterested
or relaxed.
(Can tossed)   Calm/Easygoing
Stays where he is and observes
the can. Walks slowly toward it.

Lies on the can. Plays with it. Or
he does not look at the can and
continues what he is doing.

(Can behind your back)   Aggressive
Stops. Looks at you. Makes direct   (Dominant)
eye contact. Ears erect. Hackles up.
Tail up. Aggressive stance. Barks
or growls.

(Can behind your back)   Aggressive
Backs away. Growls. Curls his lips.   (Fear)
Barks with insecurity. Crouches.
Lowers his tail. Ears down.
Submissive posture. Shows his teeth.
Wets submissively.

(No Aggressive Personality reactions entered for *Can
tossed.*)

3. Is Your Dog Hand Shy?

Reaction to Discipline Test

The purpose of this test is to determine if your puppy has
been hit or punished by a hand or a rolled-up newspaper on the
face, the rump, or any other part of the body, and how he responds to those threats. The result of hitting a dog could be the
biting of children, family members, or strangers. Hitting a dog is
one of the major causes of dog bites. This is essential information
so that you do not frighten the puppy in everyday matters, in
training, and even when offering affectionate handling. For example, when teaching the command DOWN (see Chapter Nine)
your hand must be slowly lowered past the dog's mouth. If he
has been hit in the past, this teaching gesture may cause him to
bite you. When you have visitors, the first thing they want to do

when they meet your dog is pet him. If he has been hit and yelled at, he may cower or bite them when they try to touch him.

Few dog owners realize that they could be the cause of their dog's fear of the human hand or voice. They may not associate the dog's fears with the punishments and types of discipline they have used in misguided attempts at training or solving behavior problems. Without the results of these tests they may never see the consequences of their methods. It is pointless, however, to feel guilty if this is your situation. Administering the tests and then changing the way you relate to your dog is a far more productive approach to the problem.

How to Give the Test

There are two parts to this test. Part one involves a pretended threat to the dog with the use of your hand or a newspaper. Part two involves a pretended threat with the use of your voice.

Part one involves use of the hand. Stand one or two feet from the dog, raise your hand (with or without a rolled-up newspaper) in a threatening manner, and pretend to hit the dog. Obviously, you are *not* supposed to actually hit the dog, so do not stand too close. However, make the move seem convincing so the dog can see your threatening gesture. This will give you a clear example of his response.

CAUTION: (1) This test should not be given if your dog has shown any aggressive behavior previously (growling, snarling, biting). (2) Do not give this test if your dog is over one year old and has aggressive qualities. (3) If your dog shows immediate fear, discontinue the test. You already know he is hand shy, so continuing is pointless and harmful. (4) The test should not be given more than three times. You don't want to create the very problem you are testing for. (5) Never actually strike your dog in this test, only the pretended action is important.

Part two involves use of the voice. Stand one or two feet away from the dog and yell at him in pretended anger, "Bad dog! What did you do? No! Don't you ever do that again! Never do that again! No!" Try to sound convincing. If the dog does not believe you, the test results will be useless.

Test Results

Reaction	Personality
(Use of the hand) Looks at you with curiosity. Stays in a happy frame of mind. Nips your hand playfully or actually invites you to play with him. Ignores you. Acts as if it were all a game. Eyes blink. Face is relaxed. Tail is up and wagging. Does not seem to be fazed or impressed at all. Does not respond with fear.	Responsive, Calm/Easygoing, High Energy (These are reactions of dogs of these personalities that have never been hit.)
(Use of the voice) Looks at you with curiosity. Stays in a happy frame of mind. Nips your hand playfully or actually invites you to play with him. Ignores you. Acts as if it were all a game. Eyes blink. Face is relaxed. Tail is up and wagging. Does not seem to be fazed or impressed at all. Does not respond with fear.	Responsive, Calm/Easygoing, High Energy (These are reactions of dogs of these personalities that have never been yelled at.)
(Use of the hand) Cowers in fear. Ducks his head and turns away from you. Lowers his ears and his tail. Cries out. Yelps. Tries to bite	Shy/Insecure/ Timid (These are reactions of dogs of this

your hand or the newspaper. Wets submissively. Curls his lips. Rolls over on his back. Flinches. Drops his rear end. Tucks tail under the body. Tries to run away from you. Drops to the ground quickly.

(Use of the voice) Cowers in fear. Ducks his head and turns away from you. Lowers his ears and his tail. Cries out. Yelps. Wets submissively. Curls his lips. Rolls over on his back. Flinches. Drops his rear end. Tucks tail under the body. Tries to get away from you. Drops to the ground quickly.

(Use of the hand) Growls. Curls his lips. Snarls. Bites. Acts menacing toward you. Barks aggressively. (If any of these behaviors are seen, stop the test immediately.)

(Use of the voice) Growls. Curls his lips. Snarls. Bites. Acts menacing toward you. Barks aggressively. (If any of these behaviors are seen, stop the test immediately.)

personality type that have been hit.)

Shy/Insecure/ Timid (These are reactions of dogs of this personality type that have been yelled at.)

Aggressive (Dominant) (These are reactions of dogs of this personality type that have been hit.)

Aggressive (Dominant) (These are reactions of dogs of this personality type that have been yelled at.)

(Use of the hand) Growls. Curls his lips. Tries to bite in an attempt to protect himself rather than in an aggressive attack. All the behaviors of a shy-type personality, but with added aggressiveness.

Aggressive (Fear) (These are reactions of dogs of this personality type that have been hit.)

(Use of the voice) Growls. Curls his lips. Tries to bite in an attempt to protect himself rather than in an aggressive attack. All the behaviors of a shy-type personality, but with added aggressiveness.

Aggressive (Fear) (These are reactions of dogs of this personality type that have been yelled at.)

4. How Strong Is Your Dog's Personality?

Dominant or Subordinate Test

The purpose of this test is to determine if your dog has a dominant or subordinate personality. Knowing this helps you understand how to relate to your dog. No value judgment is made here as to which type of personality is better. Whether it is better to have a dominant or subordinate type depends on personal taste and needs. A dominant-type dog may be outgoing, independent, and very likely to protect you, but he may also scare away your friends and neighbors, depending on the degree of his dominance. A subordinate dog may be very affectionate and attentive, but could be too clinging, a bit too timid. What is important is that you relate to your dog in a manner that is appropriate for his personality.

How to Give the Test

In a secluded area inside or outside your home, place your puppy on his back, lying flat. The dog must not be on his side, as if you were scratching his chest. Be sure he is on his spine. Crouch over him, straddling his body between your legs or, if necessary, kneel beside him. This is a position that makes any dog feel extremely vulnerable. Place your right hand over the part of the puppy's collar facing you and gently but firmly grab the skin under his throat. Be quiet, firm, and unresponsive to the dog's reactions. Administer this test for fifteen or thirty seconds only.

Test Results

Reaction	Personality
He lies calmly on the ground. Squirms around and tries to get up. Happy expression on his face. His entire body is relaxed. Front legs are bent in toward his chest like an infant's. Back legs are spread out and extended. He thinks this is a big game.	Responsive
Moves around a lot. Tries to get up. Resists staying in one place. Mouths your hands. Makes sounds of protest. Depending on his size, it can be quite a fun battle. Gives you a hard time just putting him on his back. Feels like a wrestling match. Eyes are happy, alert, and mischievous.	High Energy
He fights and resists. Tries to get up. Does not like being on his back. Tries to pull your hand away with his mouth. Fights with his paws. Shakes a great deal. Battles to get up. Growls. Acts very aggressively. Clearly does not want to be on his back.	Strong Willed

Reluctant to roll over, depending on the degree of his shyness or insecurity. Body is very tense and constricted. He screams or yelps or whines loudly. Sounds terrible. Eyes convey fear. His front paws try to push your hand away from him. Back legs are crunched upward. He is in a panic to get up.	Shy/Insecure/ Timid
Growls. Curls his lips. Tries to bite you. Makes direct eye contact. Does not want to be in that position.	Aggressive (Dominant)
Depending on level of fear, he growls, tries to bite and get away. He screams, yelps, or whines loudly. Body is in a submissive position. He wets. Shows all the reactions of shyness but in addition tries to bite you.	Aggressive (Fear)

5. How Tolerant Is Your Dog?

Physical Sensitivity Test

Unlike the previous tests, this one is *not* designed to establish your dog's personality type, although it does reinforce what you have already learned about that. The purpose of this test is to determine your puppy's tolerance for pain and discomfort. Understanding this aspect of his personality will help prevent dog bites.

A lack of tolerance for pain or discomfort could be inherited (the result of poor breeding), could be caused by pain-sensitive areas from physical ailments (such as hip displasia) or skin problems (such as hot spots), or could be the result of abusive behavior from humans (physical punishment).

Inexperienced pet owners often grab their dogs by the tail, the coat, and other parts of the body, and, without realizing it until it's too late, inflict a certain amount of pain. Babies, toddlers, and some thoughtless children have a tendency to pull on their dogs or even sit on them in an attempt to ride them like horses. Every dog has a different level of tolerance to physical discomfort and pain. Where one dog will tolerate the roughhouse play of a child, another will turn around and bite the child on the face. Some dogs may even continue to attack after the first bite.

The results of this test will establish your puppy's level of tolerance. It will also indicate how sensitive you must be when handling him in everyday activities and in training so that no one gets bitten. This test is concerned with the dog's comfort and the safety of humans who come in contact with him.

How to Give the Test

There are three parts of this test: (1) the tail, (2) the toes, and (3) the skin on the rump. Test your puppy in a quiet area, with no one else present. Use extreme caution if your dog is over ten months old, because his bite could be serious. Start very gently and slowly increase the level of discomfort. Use your fingers and your hands to conduct the test and control the dog with the help of a leash and collar.

The results of each test are given in two categories: Reaction, which indicates the puppy's responses to the test, and Tolerance, which indicates one of four classifications of the puppy. The four classifications are: Safe, Average, Poor, and None. If your puppy's reactions indicate he is Safe, it means he has a strong pain tolerance. If his reactions indicate he is Average, he is safe depending on how much discomfort he is exposed to. If his reactions indicate he is Poor, he could be unsafe and possibly bite. One must be cautious with such a dog. If his reactions indicate he is None, the dog is definitely unsafe and will definitely bite if not handled properly.

Part one involves the tail. Hold the dog in place with the help of a leash and collar. Grab the tail and pull it gently. Observe your dog's reactions.

Part two involves the toes. Use a leash and collar to hold the dog in place. Using your finger and thumb, press lightly between the puppy's toes, expanding them outward. Gradually increase the pressure for several seconds until the dog shows signs of discomfort.

Part three involves the skin on the rump. Use a leash and collar to hold the dog in place. With your left hand, pull the dog's skin near the rump. Pull gently at first and then increase the pressure.

Test Results

Reaction	Tolerance Level
(The tail) Looks at you. Turns around and mouths your hand. Does not seem bothered. Is comfortable. Allows you to pull on his tail. Becomes playful.	Safe
(The toes) Tolerates strong pressure for ten seconds or more. Looks at you. Licks you. Tries to get away but shows no sign of aggression. Turns it into a game.	Safe
(The skin on the rump) Skin can be pulled from gently to firmly to hard, and the dog looks at you as though it is a game. Turns around and tries to mouth your hand, but shows no signs of aggression.	Safe

(The tail) Feels comfortable with what you are doing but tries to stop you. Moves away from you or mouths your hand. Tolerates your hand for a short time. Starts to cry or whimper, but does not show any sign of aggression.	Average
(The toes) Allows you to grab toes and apply pressure for five or ten seconds. Squirms. Yelps a bit. Mouths your hands. Turns it into a game. Tries to get away. Tolerates the pain.	Average
(The skin on the rump) Allows you to pull the skin, then turns around and tries to snap at your hand, but without real aggression. Whines and cries a bit, but shows no signs of growling or biting.	Average
(The tail) Low tolerance. Yelps, howls, screams. Growls. Curls lips. Snaps. Tries to get away.	Poor (not recommended for young children)
(The toes) Cries. Screams. Yells. Tries to bite your hand. Growls. Becomes frightened and tries to run away. Will no longer allow you to touch his paws. Turns it into a battle of wills.	Poor (still a lovable puppy, but with a low pain tolerance)
(The skin on the rump) Screams. Tries to bite your hand. Growls.	Poor (not recommended for

Tries to run away. Cowers as if being hurt. Shows submissive posture or dominant aggression, depending on personality.	young children, but still a lovable dog)
(The tail) Bites and growls when tail is pulled.	None (not recommended for any children)
(The toes) Growls. Screams. No tolerance at all.	None (not recommended for any children)
(The skin on the rump) Growls and then tries to bite you. Bites without warning growls.	None (not recommended for any children)

The Six Personality Types

A Responsive type is a dog that is eager to learn, willing to please, and quick to understand. He can be handled in a normal, moderate manner with average corrections and generous praise. Leash corrections, voice corrections, and noise corrections (shake can) should be vigorous, but no more than necessary.

A High-Energy type is essentially a dog that is easily distracted and excitable. He requires firm handling, patience, and subdued use of praise to avoid getting the dog too excited. Use demanding and determined corrections on High-Energy dogs.

The Strong-Willed type is stubborn and resists the teaching process. Eventually he will do what you want, but not without a challenge. You must be assertive through the use of your voice and body language. Be patient but demanding and persistent. Use lavish praise after each correction. Vocal corrections should be loud and firm. Leash corrections should be medium to hard.

The Shy/Insecure type may be a timid or fear-ridden dog. He may be afraid of noise, sudden movements, strangers, or new situations and places. Handle such dogs with sensitivity, understanding, and patience. This personality type should only be corrected verbally, in a soft tone of voice. Do not use leash or noise corrections. Praise the dog with love, affection, and enthusiasm after each correction.

Dogs of the Calm/Easygoing type are sedate, lethargic, and live life at a slower pace than most dogs. They must be motivated to get them moving. This is accomplished by giving commands firmly, but with love and affection. Lavish praise is important. Patience and tolerance for their slow response to you does more for the teaching process than harsh corrections. Voice corrections are more effective than any other. Use a soft tone of voice and only be as firm as necessary. Never use noise corrections (shake can) for this personality type. Leash corrections are rarely needed. Use them only when absolutely necessary, and administer them in a gentle-to-firm manner.

The Aggressive type is viewed in two categories: Dominant Aggressive and Fear Aggressive. A Dominant Aggressive dog is more dangerous than any other personality type. He guards and protects his territory (and sometimes those who live in it) and considers himself the leader of his pack. Such dogs are often controlling and menacing.

A *Fear Aggressive* dog can be equally as frightening but is less dangerous. Dogs of this type are ruled by their own fears. Many shy dogs become fear aggressive, and the same is true of dogs with a phobia. This form of behavior can be inherited or developed as a result of early abuse or frightening experiences.

Aggressive dogs are usually upsetting, frightening, and sometimes dangerous. Aggressiveness in dogs is seen in various degrees as simple assertive behavior, bullying, occasional biting, and uninhibited attack behavior. When this behavior is indicated by the personality tests, special handling is necessary. Aggressive puppies ten months and under can be brought under control if trained properly. A puppy ten months and older should be evaluated by a professional dog trainer, veterinarian, or animal behaviorist before you attempt to train him yourself. The older an aggressive dog becomes, the more dangerous it is to train him.

Aggressive-type dogs require a light-to-medium leash correction, accompanied with a loud, firm voice correction. However, a dominant aggressive dog requires a hard jerk in addition to a loud, firm voice correction. Discontinue such corrections if the dog reacts violently, and seek professional help. Noise corrections are useful for the fear aggressive type but not the dominant aggressive type. A loud use of the shake can in full view of the puppy is effective for problem solving by indicating he is in the act of doing something wrong. All voice corrections should be said in a loud, firm tone of voice. Voice corrections demand the use of the word *No. Always praise your dog lavishly after each and every correction.* That tells the dog he is still in good standing with you and reinforces the teaching.

FOUR

SHOPPING SPREE: THE STUFF YOU NEED

Bringing home a puppy is very much like bringing home a new baby except for two things. No one expects you to pass out cigars and no one throws you a baby shower where your friends buy you everything from booties to bottles. You're on your own when you get a new puppy. This chapter is devoted to the things you need to make life nice and easy with your new toddler-with-a-tail.

Bedding

Your puppy deserves a comfortable bed to sleep on. When he was at the kennel, he enjoyed the warmth and protection that came from sleeping on his mother's belly while cuddling with the other baby dogs. Obviously, you cannot provide the beat of the mother's heart or the gentle movements of her breathing as the entire litter slept by her in a heap of calm and security.

But you can provide the softness, the warmth, and the comfort he once knew. If your little dog came from a source other than a kennel, then he has slept on shredded paper or cedar chips, with or without other puppies not related to him. In either case, you should provide soft, warm bedding to help him make a happy adjustment to his new life.

An old blanket or large towel is sufficient. However, there are good items that are manufactured and sold in pet-supply stores and mail-order catalogs. You can, for example, purchase blankets designed to resist the digging, chewing, and soiling behavior of puppies. There are acrylic fake-fur pet beds of all sizes and shapes. These are soft and cozy. You can buy large dog pillows with washable covers, and padded mats that are ideal for travel because they are lightweight and can be folded. There are even orthopedic dog beds and travel beds that fit into the backseat of a car and even attach to the seat belts. Whatever your decision, a family dog should have a bed of his own.

Equipment for Confinement

The new puppy needs a home within his home. If he is permitted to have the run of the house, particularly when you cannot supervise him, he is going to soil everywhere and get himself into a lot of trouble. Confinement is also an integral part of housebreaking or paper training. You cannot teach a puppy to control himself if you do not confine him to one small area. By giving him the run of the house you give him the opportunity to mark off many places with the scent of his urine and feces. This is his way of claiming his territory. He will then always return to those places and soil them again and again as a way of restaking his claim. Here is the equipment that prevents this.

Puppy Gate In order to prevent your dog from getting into trouble around your house when you're not there, you can confine him to one room. If you choose a small area and close the door on him, he may become frightened, lonely, and bored. This may cause him to bark, howl, chew destructively, or relieve himself all over the floor. This can also create separation anxiety and frantic escape behaviors that may continue for years.

You can avoid this by confining your puppy to a room that is blocked off with a puppy gate rather than a closed door. The gate allows him to see outside the room, and that makes all the difference. This allows him to watch family activities without actually being underfoot. Puppy gates are sold in hardware stores, pet-supply stores, and mail-order catalogs for pet owners. They are manufactured in wood, plastic, and metal. Most of them work with a spring mechanism that applies pressure to each side of the doorway.

Dog Crate A dog crate is a commercially manufactured enclosure. It is a collapsible cage made of strong metal wire, with a solid floor and a hinged door at the front. It is humane and extremely effective when used properly. Dog crates are used for housebreaking, paper training, problem solving, and for keeping your puppy out of trouble when you cannot supervise him. Although it is designed to confine your new dog during his period of adjustment, it later functions as an indoor doghouse with the door kept open at all times. It quickly becomes a sanctuary; a safe place to rest, retreat, and get away from it all.

Once your dog has adjusted to his home and is completely housebroken, his crate, with the door open at all times, will be a comfortable place for him when the family is away. A dog crate appeals to the canine instinct to create a den. In nature, wild dogs and wolves develop a core area in their territory, called a den, in which they sleep, rest, or retreat. Sometimes the den is a cave and sometimes it is a large hole in the ground or the hollow of a log. When you travel with your dog, the crate can be used as a portable den, providing security, comfort, and safety in a moving vehicle.

A puppy will usually accept a crate with ease if he is not placed in one with anger or as punishment. Set the crate up close to the center of family activities, such as in the kitchen or hallway. Keep it away from drafts or direct heat, and make it comfortable with a dog bed or a blanket; and put some treats inside. At night, drape a large towel or sheet over the top and sides to make it more denlike. It is *very* important to keep in mind that a puppy should not be enclosed in a dog crate with the door closed for longer than *four* hours at a time. A mature dog can remain for a longer period, but an entire day is much too long for any dog to remain in a crate. You may crate your puppy for the night providing the wire door is left *open* and the unit is in an enclosed area, such as the kitchen.

A wire dog crate should be long enough to permit your dog to stretch out and high enough for him to sit up without hitting his head. Purchase a full-size crate designed for your dog breed even though he is only a puppy now. You can fill it up with a dog bed or blanket and many toys.

Feeding Equipment

Bowls There is a wide variety of food and water bowls to choose from, and they are used in different ways. The first consideration is size. Do not use a bowl that is too large, because it could influence you to overfeed your dog. Some bowls are made for tall dogs; they sit high off the floor in a sturdy metal rack. Some bowls are shallow and flat for small dogs, while some are deeper for larger dogs. There are sizable self-feeding containers that hold large quantities of dry food; these allow dogs to eat whenever they are hungry. There are also large and small food containers that can be preset with a timer to automatically dispense a measured ration of dry dog food at designated times.

The shape of the bowl is another consideration. For example, there are bowls designed to accommodate dogs with long, floppy ears, like Cocker Spaniels. These are usually deeper than the average bowl and have a small opening with a wide bottom. They prevent the dog from getting his ears into the food or water but leave room for the length of his face. Also available is a puppy pan with a raised center, leaving a circular "trough" around the outside, allowing more than one puppy to feed at the same time. The best food and water bowls are made of stainless steel or stoneware. Some have nonskid strips on them to stop them from sliding around and a flared-out-at-the-bottom design to prevent them from tipping over. Beware of thin-gauge metal or plastic bowls that can be chewed through quite easily by an industrious puppy. This would be harmful if pieces were swallowed.

TOYS

Dog toys should be more than a source of entertainment; they should promote exercise, appeal to the dog's instinctive nature, relieve boredom, alleviate the discomfort of teething, and simply provide a dog with possessions he can claim as his own. A dog toy should relate to a dog's basic instincts. When animals (and children) play, they are learning or practicing real-life activities. A hard rubber ball rolling across the floor, for example, triggers a dog's instinct to hunt and capture his food. Although toys that squeak can capture a dog's curiosity, they are easily chewed up and therefore potentially harmful. Too often little metal bells and squeakers are chewed out of flimsy toys and swallowed by the family pet, sending him straight to the veterinarian.

Young puppies have strong, sharp teeth. They can tear apart plastic and rubber toys quite easily. Bones made of hard nylon material are better, as are some toys such as rawhide bones, which are actually meant to be destroyed; both help satisfy a dog's urge to chew. These are necessary for young dogs, between two and six months of age, that are teething, and when used properly, they can be an effective aid in solving destructive chewing problems (see Chapter Six).

When you go to purchase dog toys, be sure they are safe and well made. Avoid medical problems by throwing away old or worn toys before they fall apart and are swallowed. Before buying a toy, be certain there are no toxic materials in them, such as paint with lead. Avoid toys with small parts that can fall off and be swallowed, and remove strings and ribbons. If you have a small dog, get him a small toy, and if you have a big dog, get him a big toy. Do not buy your dog a chew toy that simulates something real in your home that you would not want chewed, such as a shoe or a book, and do not use chew toys to play pulling games with your dog. This promotes aggressive behavior and teaches your dog to nip, bite, and growl.

Grooming Tools

Brushes A *natural-bristle brush* is the universal grooming tool used for the care of both long- and short-coated dogs. It comes in a variety of sizes and shapes, with soft, medium, or stiff bristles. The one you select should depend on your dog's size, coat length, and coat texture. Consult a groomer or pet-supplies dealer.

A *pin brush* is used to groom long-coated dogs of both small and large breeds, such as Cocker Spaniels, Borzois, Afghans, and Shetland Sheepdogs. A pin brush has long or short stainless-steel or chrome-plated pins with rounded ends that are set in a soft rubber base to remain highly flexible. The pins come in short, medium, and long lengths and are selected on the basis of the length of a dog's coat.

A *slicker brush* is rectangular in shape, with a wooden handle and short, bent-wire teeth placed close together and resembling the metal fins inside an air conditioner. It is available in small, medium, and large sizes and is best for dogs with medium-length coats. Its purpose is to untangle mats and remove dead hair.

A *rubber brush* is made of one molded piece of rubber, including rubber teeth, used for grooming and polishing short-coated and smooth-coated breeds. The rubber brush can also be used for shampooing and massaging the skin without scratching or irritating sensitive dogs, but it is of absolutely no use in grooming long- or medium-coated breeds.

Combs Dog combs of stainless steel and high-quality aluminum are best. A *half-medium, half-fine comb* is useful for most breeds and coat types: The fine teeth are for soft or silky hair; the medium teeth are used for coats of average texture.

A *rake* or *matting comb* is for the fur of very heavy-coated breeds, such as the Old English Sheepdog or the Newfoundland. It helps undo twisted and matted fur and comes in several sizes, with or without a handle.

A *flea comb* is not used primarily to remove fleas. Its main use is to comb out very fine facial and leg hair, especially on silky-coated breeds, and this very fine tooth comb comes with or without a handle.

A *stripping comb* or *stripping knife* is for the stripping technique used on most terrier breeds, Schnauzers, and various other breeds. It requires a special technique for thinning the coat, removing dead hair, and for keeping the dog cool in the summer. The blade of the comb or knife has one edge serrated in fine, medium, or coarse widths. Heavy-shedding dogs benefit the most from stripping. Consult a pet supplier or professional dog groomer.

Tools for Training and Problem Solving

The Training Lead As stated in Chapter Two, obedience training should not be the first order of business with a new dog.

However, being able to control your puppy is essential, and that means getting him used to wearing a leash. The best way to do this is to purchase a lightweight *show lead,* which is made of a woven synthetic material and is worn around the neck without a collar. It has an adjustable loop made to fit any size dog with the help of a sliding plastic bead. Place it around the puppy's neck and allow him to drag it around with him for an hour at a time until he becomes accustomed to it. You may use the training lead to control your puppy until you are ready to initiate obedience training.

The Leash You will need a six-foot leather leash with a metal clip on the end for everyday use and for obedience training. *In dog training and problem solving, the leash is the primary means of teaching, correcting, and communicating with a dog.*

Although leashes can be purchased in braided nylon, nylon webbing, and metal, a six-foot leather leash is the safest, most durable type for training and everyday use. Leather softens with age, making it more comfortable for the dog and longer lasting than most other materials, and is easier on your hand as well as the dog. One can hardly tell when a metal leash is about to break, while with leather it is quite apparent, as it begins to wear and thin out. Metal leashes sometimes develop sharp edges that can irritate or scratch your dog, and while nylon webbing is very popular because of its strength, light weight, and bright colors, it can burn your hand if your dog quickly pulls away from you.

When purchasing a leather leash, get one that is five-eighths of an inch wide for a medium-to-large dog. This will provide needed strength for a large dog without overwhelming him if he is delicate or has a long coat. Wider widths can be used for very large dogs and narrower widths for smaller ones. Strength and comfort are the main considerations when selecting the proper leash for your dog.

Training Collar Next to the leash, the training collar is the most important thing you'll need. Once you learn how to place it on the dog and use it properly, you will understand what a simple but effective device it is. It is simply a length of small-link chain with a metal ring at each end, although training collars are also manufactured in leather and nylon.

You can even improvise one with the sewn loop meant for your hand at the end of any leash. Instead of hooking the metal clip to a collar, run it through the hand loop, forming a temporary lasso. Place it around the dog's neck, hold the metal clip in your hand, and pull it gently until the loop fits snugly. It works well in an emergency if the collar breaks. You can use this to catch a dog that has gotten away from you, because it will tighten around a dog's neck as you pull it. Bear in mind that this should only be used as a temporary collar. A manufactured training collar is a necessity if you hope to train your dog or solve any of his behavior problems.

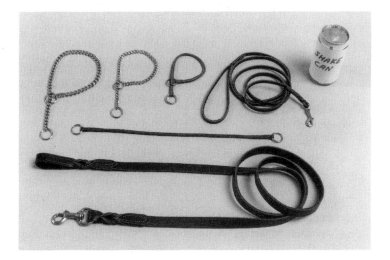

The training collar must be attached to the six-foot leather leash. When used properly, the leash is pulled to the side, causing the collar to gently tighten around the dog's neck for a split second. It must then be released instantly. Its purpose is to communicate to the dog through a mild sensation and metallic sound the message that he did the wrong thing, but it is not a punishment device. The training collar is a correction device and does not hurt the dog. Remember: Verbal praise must always follow such a correction.

The training collar is the most effective, kindest, and most humane training device available. It is easier on a dog than a very harsh tone of voice and far more communicative. Without it one could not train a dog properly or solve many of the behavior problems that spring up.

Your training collar should be made of small, highly polished metal links made of stainless steel or high-quality aluminum. The best training collars are referred to as "jeweled." At each end of the chain is a solid metal ring. The chain slips through one ring, forming a loop, and the leash is attached to the remaining ring. If your dog has very fine or silky hair, use a leather or nylon training collar, as a metal collar could rub some of the coat away. Leather and nylon are more suitable for small or fragile dogs.

Size is an important consideration as well. When the collar is too long, it becomes too heavy for the dog, and the leash corrections become ineffective. By adding three inches to the circumference of your dog's neck, you will come up with a number that is your dog's correct collar size. (See Chapter Nine to learn how to place the collar on the dog and how to execute a leash correction.)

Shake Can The shake can is a homemade device that is easy to make and costs nothing. It is an effective corrective tool that can be placed all over the house and used whenever the dog is not wearing his leash and collar.

You can make as many shake cans as you need by taking empty soda cans, washing them out, and putting enough pennies inside to make noise when the can is shaken. Close the opening with tape so the pennies cannot fall out. When you shake these cans, they rattle loudly like a party favor. By rattling a shake can and saying "No" in a loud tone of voice, you easily command a dog or puppy's attention and let him know that he is doing something wrong. You can add this to your arsenal of training corrections. However, it is important to understand that not every dog should be corrected with a shake can. For example, many shy dogs become too upset with this or any other harsh correction. It is important to know your dog well and decide whether this form of correction is appropriate. If your dog becomes aggressive or cowers severely when the shake can is used, then discontinue all corrections with it.

Identification

I.D. Tag There are several ways you can lose your dog; he can be lost, stolen, or the unfortunate victim of mistaken identity. The simplest and most convenient form of prevention is the metal I.D. tag, which can be purchased in a pet-supply store or through a mail-order pet catalog. You pay for the tag in advance, fill out a form, and send it in. Within a short period of time the customized tag is sent to you in the mail.

Some things to keep in mind, however: The etched information on metal tags eventually wears down and becomes hard to read. The tag may also work its way off the collar or become snagged on a protrusion that your dog rubs against. Some quality leather collars have a metal I.D. plate fixed to them, and when engraved with the correct identifying information these plates are far more effective than the dangling type. Never rely on a rabies tag (obtained from your veterinarian) or a metal dog license as a form of identification, as this license is an effective form of I.D. for your local pound but useless to anyone else.

I.D. Tattoo There is probably no better method of identifying a dog than having him tattooed inside his right, hind thigh. The tattoo is painless, humane, inexpensive, and very effective. Many veterinarians can perform this service for you or at least guide you to someone who can. There are several national dog registries that not only apply the tattoo but also keep your dog's identification tattoo on file so that he can be returned to you if necessary. These organizations give you a tag to place on the dog's neck with all the pertinent information for anyone who happens to find your dog. There can be no doubt as to the ownership of a dog when it is tattooed with the owner's name, Social Security number, or other personal form of I.D.

Dog Clothes

Coats, Sweaters, Shirts There is only one important reason for animals to wear manufactured clothing and that is to keep them warm and dry. Some dogs cannot maintain good health when exposed to weather conditions that are too harsh for them. Most pets cannot tolerate prolonged exposure to the cold, and even dogs that live outdoors are in jeopardy if they remain in zero-degree temperature for extended periods of time. This is especially true for puppies, aging animals, those in poor health, and dogs with shorthaired coats. Some veterinarians even approve of galoshes for city dogs. They protect the paws from pain caused by de-icing salt and other chemicals spread over the streets and sidewalks after heavy snows. Raincoats for some dogs are also very much in order.

When looking for a garment to keep your dog warm, choose one that fits snugly on the body, especially over the belly. Dog coats and sweaters are available everywhere and are usually found in blanket-weight materials that are warm enough when the dog is exposed to cold weather for short periods of time. A good dog coat should be lined with a water-resistant or waterproof material. Sweaters are best in the turtleneck variety. When going out in bad weather here is the only rule to follow: If your dog looks cold, chances are he is cold.

FIVE

DOG BEHAVIOR: WHY THEY DO WHAT THEY DO

If you don't understand your puppy now, how are you ever going to cope with him when he grows into a full-size dog? Your puppy is not a four-legged house plant that you can water and watch grow as he waits patiently to be placed in the sun. Like all animals, dogs instinctively behave in special ways that are unique. *A dog's gotta do whatta dog's gotta do.* He is a remarkable, often misunderstood animal.

The Parent Trap

When you get a puppy, you assume the role of parent and guardian for the life of the animal, and as the puppy matures he becomes more like a friend, certainly a loyal companion. Although he remains totally dependent on you throughout his life, he does earn the status of a full-fledged family member. Considering how long your relationship is going to be, it is a good idea to come to terms with his doggieness. That means learning what is normal behavior *for a dog.* When you understand the fundamentals of canine behavior, your ability to communicate with your pet becomes greatly enhanced. The miracle of dog/human communication is no different from communication between different peoples. It is based on knowledge, understanding, and tolerance. Here then is an abbreviated primer on the basics of canine behavior. It is by no means complete, but the most important aspects of dog behavior that influence our ability to understand dogs are here.

Two of a Kind

Much of what is known about domestic dogs stems from the similarities in basic behavior of dogs and wolves. Dogs, like wolves, are canids, members of the family Canidae. These two species have many behavior traits in common, the most striking being that they live in a pack or small community.

The Pack

The pack can be likened to a nation that works together and strives to make life safe and prosperous for all its citizens. In order to achieve these goals, everyone must play a part and serve some function. You could also think of a pack as a loose-knit family.

Canids develop a social order based on strength, ferocity, and leadership abilities. Once the social order is established, the pack goes about the business of defending territory, finding prey, and securing food by bringing down the stray and dying members of the prey herds. Mating takes place, cubs or puppies are born, and they are raised, fed, and protected. The pack constantly replenishes itself with a new, young population, and life goes on. This all happens within the discipline of a demanding social structure. Pack behavior establishes the need to be with other creatures, and when living as pets, dogs transfer this need to humans. The family, even if this consists of just you and the dog, is then viewed as a substitute pack by the dog. This explains why dogs are constant and loyal companions. Whether in the wild or at the feet of the humans they live with, dogs form strong social attachments and are capable of developing and maintaining many intense and complex relationships, to the extent that some would sacrifice their lives for their families. Some have.

If you examine the social structure of the wolf pack, you will understand the basic instincts of your family dog. Sometimes wolf packs are made up of blood relations and sometimes combinations of relatives and close neighbors who join them. Establishing a territory, hunting in that territory, and defending the territory from intruders, which are the essentials for survival in the wild, are accomplished as a group effort.

Who's the Boss?

In a wolf pack, there is a chain of command established that involves a leader of the pack and the lower ranking wolves in the pecking order. In order for the pack to function, it must exist with a minimum of conflict within its ranks. Battles within the pack are kept to a minimum by the natural tendency toward being a leader or a follower. The leader is determined by size, strength, ferocity, and by his ability to fight. Once the lead wolf (or alpha wolf) is determined, the lower-ranking wolves sort themselves out and assume various responsibilities and privileges based on their rank.

These basic instincts and the behaviors they create are ingrained in every puppy from birth, and entering into a human/canine home does not change this. Puppies merely transfer the need for pack structure to the human situation and turn the idea of "pack" into the one more familiar to us—"family." His instinct is to either lead the family or be led by the strongest member(s). From the dog's point of view, a leader is absolutely necessary, and the dog's instinct for survival forces him to fill the position of leader if no member of the human family takes on the responsibility. It is necessary that a family pet be given the status of subordinate family member rather than the dominant member or he will never be trained. If you carefully observe the behavior of the most timid or the most aggressive house dog, you will see this pattern in action.

Family Ties

All dogs instinctively adhere to a social structure of dominance and subordination. This is the single most important fact for every new puppy owner to know. When you bring home a puppy, he will eventually attempt to run the household unless you clearly establish yourself as the leader of his pack. Dogs accept leadership from those with dominant personalities or those who behave with some degree of authority. Once you assume the position of leadership, the young dog accepts it for the rest of his life. This should be the relationship between the dog and every other member of the household.

It is not necessary for one to throw his or her weight around with a dog and act like a petty tyrant, as human authority is already established by size, tone of voice, taking charge, and insisting on good behavior. Some owners are reluctant to take this stance with their dogs, as they are either afraid of their pets or fear they will alienate them. Fear can best be overcome by taking charge and becoming the dog's leader. A professional dog trainer can be very useful in that situation. As for alienation of affection, it is important to understand that you will never lose the love of your dog, because you are the leader of his pack. On the contrary, he will become more attached to you than ever for assuming command.

Hold Me, Hold Me, Hold Me

It is now widely accepted that there are critical phases in the earliest weeks of a puppy's life that help shape his ability to easily adapt to humans, other dogs, and new situations. The first three weeks of a puppy's life are spent developing his ability to walk, to see, and to hear. Between the fourth and thirteenth weeks, his adaptability to other living beings is determined if certain conditions are present in the puppy's immediate environment. Isolation or lack of human attention during this period will not permit the animal to develop an adaptability to humans or other dogs.

A happy dog, responsive to humans, is one that is held and touched as a puppy.

A dog kept exclusively with other dogs and never introduced to humans during this stage will adapt only to the presence of other dogs throughout its life. If the dog is exposed to humans every day and handled fondly by them during this critical period (three to twelve weeks), he will become extremely adaptable to humans, family life, and obedience training. This is called socializing, as mentioned in Chapter One.

Between seven and sixteen weeks of age the puppy enters the period when he is most adaptive to living with humans and is also ready to develop a dominant or subordinate role in his pack or family. Obedience training is more effective and easier to accomplish at this time in the puppy's life than at any other stage.

Teacher's Pet

Wild dogs and wolves take excellent care of their young. They nurse and wean their puppies, and for a long period of time they will bring freshly killed meat to the den, where the hungry cubs eagerly wait for their meal. Once the young are old enough, they are taken on hunting expeditions and taught how to track, kill, and feed off prey animals. In the domestic dog's case, humans are the substitute parents and perform all these nurturing services. Male wolves are as involved in the giving of care and attention to the cubs as are the females and often take over some of the responsibilities of rearing the young. In a pack society, "aunts" and "uncles" also help in feeding and looking after the cubs.

Even though an order of dominance and subordination begins to develop within the litter itself, it is quite clear that a cub's or puppy's position within the larger pack structure is definitely a subordinate one. No adult dog or wolf would tolerate the least bit of insubordination from a pup without some form of reprimand, such as a cuff on the muzzle or carrying the offender off by the scruff of his neck.

Things Change

Not until the dominant wolf is older and weaker does the younger member of the pack get his way. At this time, an old or sick member of the pack loses his position by a physical challenge that often results in his death. Old or widowed wolves whose teeth are no longer sharp enough to fight or hunt often become "lone wolves" and live away from the pack, eating what they can scavenge from the leftovers. For these reasons, a change of status is much feared. When there are too many wolves in the pack for their territory, some of the younger ones break away and form their own pack and look for another place to establish territory.

A Dog for the People

The most desirable lifestyle for a dog lies between the boundaries of his instinctive behavior and the needs and conditions set up by his human family. Dog behavior is, in most instances, a modified version of wolf behavior. When a small puppy leaves his litter and moves into a human environment, he simply transfers his pack behavior to the new environment and relates to his human family as to another dog or wolf pack. This works perfectly because of the compatibility between family life and pack behavior. As stated earlier, in human families as in wolf packs, a social structure based on dominant-subordinate relationships is developed with unusual clarity. The dog's behavior even takes on whatever colorations exist in the human situation. Human attitudes toward animals and human neuroses seem to have an important influence on a dog's behavior. Basic obedience training makes dogs manageable but does not necessarily alter any distorted behavior tendencies.

Have you ever witnessed a Dachshund having a psychosomatic asthma attack? The poor dog hacks and wheezes and honks in situations where he cannot have his own way. Fat dogs that eat until their eyes cross overeat as a ploy to get attention or because they fear they'll never be fed again. Some dogs deliberately disobey commands and the rules of good conduct as a form of protest, or because they are imitating what they see around them.

There are dogs that pace, dogs that suffer from insomnia, dogs that fear strangers, dogs that fear other dogs, dogs that are sexually attracted to humans, and even dogs that suffer mental breakdowns. Dogs, in their current state of domestication, are subject to almost all the distortions of behavior found in humans. When neurotic behavior of the human variety is seen in dogs, you can be sure it comes from the family the dog lives with, even though they are the ones most upset by it.

What helps is understanding what is normal for a dog and what is neurotic or, more accurately, problematic for human beings. For example, a dog is not neurotic because he is difficult to housebreak and continually soils the floor. He is simply untrained and unprepared to satisfy human expectations. In his natural state, he uses his urine and feces to claim territory and establish his boundaries. He urinates on trees, rocks, inside caves, and wherever he wants his presence known. Some of the most troubling things that dogs do are actually quite natural and normal, for dogs. It simply means they have to be corrected at the appropriate time and in the appropriate manner so that they can live successfully in a human environment. Fair or not, dogs find themselves in the uncomfortable position of being forced to adjust *their* behavior to human conditions. It is important for the caring puppy person to understand the difference and not lose patience.

Most so-called dog problems are not problems at all in a dog's own, natural environment. This includes chewing, begging, howling, digging, fighting, jumping, stealing (food), even mounting, snarling, and biting. Although this is no answer to a dog owner's prayers, it offers some consolation until the correct solution is found. The solution lies with bonding, understanding something about dog behavior, determining your dog's temperament, correcting his problem behavior, obedience training, and giving him all the love and care that he needs.

SIX

THE PUPPY OWNER'S
QUICK-FIX
PROBLEM SOLVER

"Help! I just got a puppy. What do I do?" That is the near-hysterical cry heard by dog trainers everywhere from new puppy owners almost every day of the week. As the fantasy of living with a cuddly puppy becomes a reality, the sweet dream turns into an absurd fact. How do you live with an insistent little rogue that yipes all night, runs around your house out of control, refuses to walk with you outdoors, pees and poops everywhere, and gnaws at your big toe?

If you can't get the authors to come to your home and teach

you how to make friends and influence dogs, this chapter is the next best thing. The immediate problems of puppyhood are temporary and can be resolved with this *Quick-Fix* Problem Solver, which encourages you to get rid of the problem, not the dog. Troublesome puppy behavior will not usually develop into major dog problems as the animal matures. This is especially true if the dog is obedience trained. Unless a dog's bad behavior is inherited or is caused by abuse, almost all puppy problems stem from a lack of maturity, experience, or obedience training. Most puppy problems disappear as the youngster grows into an adult dog. Time is on your side. But if a puppy drives you crazy, can you wait until he grows out of it? No, you cannot. Besides, some problem behavior becomes permanent if it is not nipped in the bud.

The Puppy Owner's *Quick Fix* Problem Solver is a digest of puppy problems and their immediate solutions. It is an important reference tool for the good, the bad, and the new dog owner. The Problem Solver helps you deal with aggravating puppy behavior quickly and efficiently.

Using the Problem Solver is easy. Simply look for the category (listed alphabetically) of your puppy's problem, such as "Chewing" or "Excessive Barking," and glance through the headings within the category to find the answer to your puppy problem. You are advised to read through the entire category section for a more thorough understanding. In addition to finding solutions to the problems, you will find a wealth of background information and some preventive strategies.

All Through the Night

When Your Puppy Cries, Yipes, and Howls All Night

A puppy cries through the night because he is frightened. He has been taken away from the comfort and security of his mother and his littermates. One of the best solutions for this problem is to keep the little dog in your room at night, in a dog crate with the gate closed. For more about dog crates, see Chapter Four, page 59. Leave a dim light on all night, and make your puppy comfortable with an old towel or blanket. Fill a hot-water bottle with warm water, wrap it in a soft towel, and place it in the dog crate next to the puppy. This will simulate the warm, sleeping bodies of his mother and littermates. Do not holler at the dog if he continues to cry. Be patient and understanding and comfort your dog with a soothing tone of voice and an occasional pat on the head. Move the crate close to your bed so he can hear you breathe as you sleep. Night crying does not last very long, and if it does not end after the first week, have the dog examined by a veterinarian for a medical problem.

Begging

Your Puppy Won't Stop Begging for Food

Believe it or not, begging is essentially a "people problem." A new puppy is as irresistible as a new baby, and everyone wants to hold him, cuddle him, and *feed him tidbits from their hands.* This progresses to feeding the little dog from the dinner table, which in turn creates his habit of being under the table whenever you sit down. Dropping bits of food onto the floor for the dog is an extension of feeding him tidbits from your hand. Eventually, the family either tires of feeding the dog during mealtime or has been served a terrific dinner and does not want to share it. When they ignore him he whimpers, whines, and, if he is large enough, places his paws on your lap or even on the table and looks at your food longingly. Some dogs, if they are big enough and bold enough, will even swipe morsels off the plate the minute you look away.

All this can be avoided by establishing a place for the dog to eat that is away from the family dining area, by not feeding him scraps of human food (especially from the table), and by not allowing the dog in the dining area during mealtimes.

How to Stop the Dog from Begging at the Table

One effective method for stopping your puppy from begging at the table is to use the commands SIT and SIT-STAY. The command SIT stops the dog from continuing what he is doing by placing him in a sitting position. However, you must give the SIT-STAY command immediately afterward if he is going to remain in that position until you release him. Other commands that are equally effective are DOWN and DOWN-STAY. These are commands that teach a dog to remain in place while you are eating. To learn how to teach these commands, see Chapter Nine.

Chewing

Why Dogs Chew

Dogs chew because: (1) their teeth hurt, (2) it feels good, (3) they are anxiety ridden, (4) they do not get enough exercise, (5) they are hungry, (6) chewing has become a habit, or (7) they are bored to death.

You Punished Your Dog After You Came Home and Found That He Chewed Up Your Carpet

It is useless to punish a dog *after the fact*. All that does is scare him and confuse him. If the dog chews the carpet (or anything else) use the alum paste solution as described on page 81. Your options for solving this problem are to (1) confine the dog when you are not home, (2) use the alum paste, or (3) correct the dog when you *catch him in the act*. See Chapter Nine for the proper method of correcting a puppy.

Eventually Puppies Stop Chewing

Normal chewing problems in dogs occur from the ages of six weeks to six months, and teething is the primary cause. It involves new, permanent teeth cutting through the gums, making the dog's mouth sore and itchy, and it is the primary reason for destructive chewing in puppies. Once the dog has finished teething, his need to chew is usually gone. However, if the puppy is not corrected properly when he chews on valuable objects, it becomes a permanent form of behavior.

You can eliminate or reduce the chewing problem by soothing your puppy's sore mouth. Soak six washcloths in cold water, squeeze them damp, twist them, and place them in your freezer overnight. Give them to the puppy to chew on, one at a time. The icy cloth temporarily numbs the pain and makes the chewing productive for the dog, but harmless for you. A plate of ice cubes can also be effective. Another method is to rub bacon fat on small-to-medium-size rawhide bones, heat them in a low oven for twenty minutes, and give them to the dog to chew on.

Your Puppy Chewed the Sofa When You Weren't Home

Prevention is the first line of defense for chewing problems. When you are not home, your young dog should be confined to one area, such as your kitchen. A store-bought puppy gate or a metal dog crate is good for confining a dog. (See pages 58–59 for more on puppy gates and dog crates.) A puppy can spend the entire night in a dog crate. It is not a good idea, however, to isolate your dog in a basement or garage, especially one that is unheated in the winter or uncooled in the summer, without the company of other dogs. Isolation can create many more problems than it might solve, as dogs are social animals that require the company of their "pack" or family.

The Bad Taste Technique

Most chewing problems end when the object of your puppy's affection tastes bad. Obtain a package of alum powder from a pharmacy and mix a small quantity with water until it reaches a pasty consistency. Smear the alum paste on anything the puppy has chewed, such as furniture legs, baseboards, or books, and allow the paste to dry. (The paste will wash off easily when you no longer need it.) If the puppy returns to the scene of the crime, he will not enjoy his chewing pastime. The alum paste, which has a terrible flavor, will serve as a self-teaching lesson that chewing unauthorized objects is a bad idea. Keep reapplying the paste every day until you are convinced the problem is over.

The Balloon Method

If the puppy likes to jump on the sofa and chew on it, try this aversion technique. Blow up many small-to-medium-size balloons. Prick one balloon with a needle close to the dog so that the loud pop startles him. Do it again. Tape the rest of the balloons to the sofa and leave. If all goes according to plan the puppy will associate the balloons with the unpleasant noise and stay away from that area. Do not use this technique if your dog is shy. (See Chapter Three to determine your dog's personality type.)

Your Puppy Only Chews When You Are Out of the House

When you are home, the dog has you to play with, to watch, to listen to, to smell. You are interesting to him, and you also make him feel more secure with your presence. When you are home, there is always the chance that you will pay attention to him. When you are not home, he becomes bored and gets into mischief, just like every other puppy. Do not take it personally.

You Tell Your Puppy "No" When He's Chewing, and He Doesn't Listen to You

Saying "No" is not always an effective method of stopping a puppy from doing what he wants to do unless he has been trained to stop. In a dog obedience course, NO is a specific command that is taught as part of the *correction* process. Formal corrections are required to stop a puppy or adult dog from misbehaving and may involve a jerk of the leash, a rattling of a shake can, or the command NO. See Chapter Nine for more about training.

You Give Your Puppy Toys and Bones, but He Still Prefers to Chew on You

Puppies love to chew, mouth, and bite anything, including parts of your body. If your puppy chews on you, it may be caused by too much carrying him around in your arms or holding him on your lap. This would give him access to your arms, legs, fingers, or even your hair. Do not carry or hold the little dog to excess, because it encourages him to chew (and to jump up on the furniture). Make it a habit to properly correct the puppy when he chews on any part of you or anyone else. For more about corrections, see Chapter Nine.

One form of correction is to keep the dog on the floor, play with him, and when he chews on your hand, give him a gentle squirt with a water gun. Say "No!" That will startle him as he begins to chew and will stop his action. Praise the dog lavishly for responding properly.

Your Other Dog Didn't Chew. What's Wrong with This Puppy?

Each dog is different and has its own personality. It is a mistake to compare one dog to another. Behavior varies from breed to breed and, to a lesser extent, from dog to dog within each breed. A puppy that chews is quite normal, even if his behavior is undesirable. Your only concern should be to correct the problem.

You Feel Guilty for Confining Your Puppy, but He's Chewing You Out of House and Home

Guilt is a *people problem*, not a *dog problem*. If you want to find your house intact when you come home, you are advised to confine your puppy in a room (such as the kitchen) behind a puppy gate, or in a metal dog crate. Make sure the crate is the correct size for your dog and is not used for excessive lengths of time. (See Chapter Four, pages 58–59, for more about gates and crates.)

Four hours is the maximum time a dog should spend in a wire crate, two to three hours for a puppy. Do not isolate your dog in a basement or a garage, especially one that is unheated or uncooled, without the company of other dogs. Confining your dog to one room (behind a see-through gate) while you are gone will not hurt the dog, and you will both be happier because he will not be able to chew anything.

Your Dog Chews Out of Spite

Spite is a conscious, human desire to harm another person, usually based on revenge or resistance to one or more persons. Dogs are much nicer than that. Spite is exclusively a human characteristic and has never been attributed to dogs as part of their basic behavior by researchers. When a puppy (or an adult dog) chews destructively, it has nothing to do with "getting even" with you. Chewing is the expression of some canine need.

When Your Puppy Is Left Behind a Door, He Seems to Chew Much More

Being left behind a closed door often causes a puppy to panic. He becomes scared, frightened and emotionally distressed because he does not know where you are. Dogs, like wolves, are highly social animals. They were born with the need to live in packs. This situation creates *separation anxiety*, which is caused by depriving a dog of his natural need to be with his "pack" or family. Confining a puppy behind a closed door is equivalent to locking a child in a closet. He may scratch furiously at the door and then chew anything available. In this situation, chewing is a desperate form of escape behavior. Obviously, you must never leave a dog in a room with a closed door. Use a see-through puppy gate or a metal dog crate. (See Chapter Four, pages 58–59.) Keeping a light on and turning on the radio when you leave will possibly ease your dog's fears and thus help to eliminate his chewing problem.

You Give Your Puppy Real Shoes and Clothes to Chew On

This is a bad idea and should not be done. If you give your puppy old shoes, he is definitely going to chew on your new shoes. He cannot discriminate between your discarded stuff and your good stuff. To a dog, stuff is stuff. You must teach him the difference between what is acceptable to chew and what is not. Give him a variety of attractive, appealing chew toys, such as nylon or rawhide bones. Never give him an object that resembles something you wouldn't want in his mouth, even if it is a dog toy, such as a latex shoe or rolled-up newspaper.

Punishing Your Dog for Chewing

Hitting your puppy with your hand or an object (such as a rolled-up newspaper) because he has chewed something is wrong for several reasons. First, it is unkind and inhumane. Second, it weakens the bond you have established. Third, it is ineffective; such methods only frighten a dog and create in him a fear of you and your hands. Chewing is normal puppy behavior. It should be corrected with positive techniques involving a leash and collar, a spray bottle, or a water gun (see Chapter Nine for more about corrections), and redirected to chew toys or frozen washcloths. It is important that your puppy associate your hands with praise and affection and *nothing else*.

The Dog Crazies

When You Let Your Puppy Out, He Runs All Over the House and Jumps on Everything

The normal response of any puppy after being let out of a confined space is to jump and run around all over the place. It is a release of his pent-up energy, and he is simply happy and very excited to be set loose. The way to prevent him from creating damage is to limit the space he has to run around in. Never give him the run of the house. Even when you release him from a small area, he should be restricted to a larger area where he has a limited amount of space in which to let out his energy.

When You Open the Door, He Runs Outside and Won't Come Back In

More than likely this is the behavior of an untrained puppy. When the door opens and he runs out, he thinks being outside is the greatest thing in the world. Maybe he won't come back in because of the way you are calling him. The tone of your voice may be too harsh, but the solution to this problem is very easy. Before opening the door, be certain the puppy is on a leash and collar. This will give you the means to retrieve the little escape artist or, perhaps, prevent him from leaving in the first place.

He Barks When You Are in the House and He's Confined

In this situation, the young puppy is lonely, misses his family, and wants attention. The answer is to be certain you are confining him properly. Never confine a puppy or a grown dog in a small room with the door closed. If you use a see-through puppy gate or a wire dog crate, it will satisfy his need to know what's going on by being able to see, hear, and smell the family activities. (For more about confinement equipment, see page 58.) Also, be sure the dog is getting enough exercise and attention.

He Runs Back and Forth Outside, Barking at the Neighbors

If the dog is outdoors most of the time, he is doing what comes naturally. He needs to be corrected whenever he indulges in this behavior. You will have to go outside and administer leash corrections with the appropriate tone of voice. (See Chapter

Nine for more about training your puppy.) He is not going to stop unless you teach him that he cannot behave that way. If you do not deal with this behavior early on, you may eventually have problems with your neighbors.

He Jumps in the Front Seat of the Car and Won't Sit Still

For safety's sake we urge you to restrain your dog and confine him to one area of your car. The consequences would be too dangerous if your dog were to jump into the front seat while you were driving.

Examine the safety equipment that is available for dogs traveling in cars. You can choose from among a wide variety of harnesses, seat belts, and dog crates. There are even dog crates designed with a slanted back to fit into a station wagon or car with a hatchback. Such equipment is available from pet-supply stores, some hardware stores, and from most mail-order, pet-supply catalogs. (See page 59 for more about dog crates.)

When You Feed Him, He Barks and Jumps All Over You

A hungry puppy gets so excited that he can't wait to eat. You can correct this problem by teaching him the commands SIT and STAY. (For more about commands, see Chapter Nine.) Once the dog has learned them, give him the proper commands and make sure he waits for the food.

When He Grabs Your Clothes, He Runs Away, Won't Let Go, Won't Drop Them

Obviously, the best solution is to prevent him from grabbing your clothes by not making them available. The alternative is to alter the puppy's behavior with a leash correction. (See Chapter Nine for more about training your puppy.) Keep the leash and collar on the dog and wait for him to grab something. When he does, correct him so he knows it's wrong.

When You Walk Him, He Tangles You Up with the Leash

When walking with your dog, the proper place for him is on your left side, with little or no slack in the leash. Talk to him as you walk so that he pays attention to you. That is the easiest way to solve the problem. Of course, he should be taught the command HEEL, which teaches him to walk with you on his best behavior. (For more about commands, see Chapter Nine.)

When You Take Him to the Vet, He Won't Stop Barking at the Other Pets

A leash correction is the proper way to end this problem (see Chapter Nine). A quick correction with a leash and collar is the simplest way to teach your dog good manners.

When You Have Company, He Won't Leave Them Alone

It is every dog owner's responsibility to see that their pet is well mannered and obedient. Once again, puppies and adult dogs learn what to do through obedience training. A simple leash correction administered whenever the puppy behaves in an unacceptable manner eventually ends most problems. In this situation, commanding your dog DOWN and STAY will solve the problem. If the dog is too much of a problem, confine him in another area behind a see-through puppy gate or in a dog crate. (See page 58 for more about confinement equipment.)

Eating

Your Puppy Doesn't Eat When You First Bring Him Home

If your puppy doesn't eat during the first couple of days, he may be having a hard time adjusting to his new home. An environmental transition is difficult and so is traveling, whether your puppy arrived via an airplane or a taxi. Take him to a veterinarian if there are medical signs, such as diarrhea or sluggishness. Be patient and understanding, and concentrate on creating a bond between the little dog and his new family. See Chapter Two for more about bonding.

Your Puppy Continues to Refuse His Food

Puppies do most of their growing in their first year. Proper growth rate and long-term good health are influenced by the quality and quantity of their food; their nutritional requirements are critical. The growing dog's body demands a larger number of nutrients per pound of body weight than the average adult dog. *For that reason it is best to feed a puppy a commercial dog food that has been formulated especially for puppies.* For more information, consult a veterinarian.

A General Rule for Dealing with the Problem

In most cases, a dog's lack of appetite is a temporary condition and must not be turned into a major problem by hand-feeding or an obsessive concern with diet. Select a premium-quality dog food and offer it in amounts recommended by your veterinarian. If your dog refuses to eat the food, he may simply not be hungry that day, or he may not like something about the food, the bowl, the kitchen, or the color of your curtains. Assuming the dog is not ill or convalescing from a recent ailment, take away the bowl after fifteen minutes and give him nothing else (except water) until his next scheduled feeding. Eventually, he will eat the fine commercial dog food you place in front of him. Do not make a fuss or call too much attention to the situation with entreaties to eat. That can only worsen matters. If the dog shows absolutely no interest in what is in his bowl, you might try making it more interesting. Add a little cottage cheese, rice, chicken or beef bouillon, or garlic powder. Be patient. Consult your veterinarian if necessary.

If Your Puppy Won't Eat, He May Be Sick

Look for medical signs, such as diarrhea, vomiting, parasites in the stool, lethargy, or anything out of the ordinary. If you suspect the dog is ill, talk to a veterinarian immediately.

If Your Puppy Won't Eat, He May Be Stressed

Puppies left alone for long periods of time become distressed because the canine nature requires a family or pack environment. Many things in the little dog's environment could stress him, such as another animal bullying him, or an overenthusiastic child. Often if you relieve the dog's stress, his appetite will return.

If Your Puppy Won't Eat, He May Be Too Upset

A dog with a nervous temperament may require a quiet, secluded place in which to eat. Eating where noise, children, or hyperactivity are present could make a nervous dog too upset to eat. Some dogs, like some people, need to be left alone to quietly enjoy their meals.

How Much to Feed Your Puppy

Quantity depends on the individual requirements of your dog, based on his breed, size, weight, temperament, lifestyle (indoor or outdoor dog), weather, and other factors. Consult your veterinarian.

How Often to Feed Your Puppy

If a puppy is under three months of age, feed him four times a day. From three to six months of age, feed him three times a day. From six months to one year old feed him twice a day. Dogs past one year should be fed once a day. However, it is a good idea to ask your veterinarian about the requirements of your own dog.

Hand-Feeding Your Dog

Try to avoid this practice if possible. Never hand-feed your dog unless your veterinarian advises you to do so. From a behavioral point of view, it creates a situation that eventually becomes intolerable and difficult to eliminate. Be consistent; create one special place to feed your dog, and always place his food and water there.

When to Give Your Puppy "People Food"

Never. Well, hardly ever. Leftovers, scraps, and food from your table could upset your dog's stomach, give him diarrhea, and most certainly make housebreaking difficult, if not impossible. Our suggestion is to stay with a premium dog food.

When to Give Your Puppy Snacks

You can give your puppy snacks after the housebreaking or paper training program is over. You can give him snacks because you love him, because he's doing the right thing, or because he's nice and is probably obedient. But please do not give your little dog snacks during his house training.

Your Dog Is Bored with Dog Food

Your dog is not bored with dog food, but *you* may be bored with giving him dog food. That is a big difference. If your dog does not eat the commercial dog food that you are giving him, try another brand. If he still refuses his ration, consult a veterinarian.

How to Feed Your Dog During Housebreaking or Paper Training

Feed your dog a quality cereal-type commercial dog food or a "balanced" wet food from a can. An important factor is consistency. Do not switch types of food or brands of food during this time. Feed the dog the same thing every day. However, the most important aspect of feeding during housebreaking is the schedule. Feed your dog the same amount at the same times every day. See Chapters Seven and Eight for more details on feeding schedules.

Feeding Your Puppy from the Dinner Table

If you begin this practice, you will be teaching your puppy to beg at your table for the rest of his life. Although it may seem cute now, it gets very annoying for you and your dinner guests once the dog grows into an adult. You have a place to eat. Your dog has a place to eat. You should keep them separate.

If begging is a problem for you (and it isn't for some), then never allow your puppy to play under the table at mealtimes. It is the same as teaching him to beg, borrow, or steal food. Bear in mind that begging might not be as tolerable to your dinner guests as it is to you. If begging is a problem for you, then you must never feed your dog from the table.

Excessive Barking

How to Stop Your Dog from Barking Excessively

Excessive barking is a problem that may require the owner to make some adjustments in the dog's lifestyle. These are covered below. However, the problem is most often solved with the use of the correction/praise method (see Chapter Nine for more complete information). Do not lose sight of the fact that barking is normal dog behavior, but excessive barking is not.

If you do *not* want your dog to bark at all, then correct him as he does it. The instant he starts to bark, say "No" in a loud, demanding tone of voice and administer a leash correction. Praise him for stopping.

If you would like your dog to bark at strangers or at noises but only for a short period of time, do not correct him for the first ten, twenty, or thirty seconds, or however long you would like him to bark before he stops. Execute a leash correction, but do *not* use the word *No*. Use the word *Cut* instead, in a demanding but not harsh tone of voice. In the language of dog training, "No" means the dog did something wrong and he must stop it immediately. "Cut" tells him to simply stop barking, that he did a good job. It is a very important distinction to the dog, and he will understand the difference if your tone of voice, body language, and attitude are firm but not harsh.

An excessive barker may require many corrections, using a training collar and a leash. (See Chapter Nine to learn how to properly execute a leash correction.)

Keep the training collar and the leash on the dog during the time you know he will bark. Have someone ring the doorbell, or simply wait for the dog to bark at something. When the dog begins to bark, take hold of the leash and jerk it quickly to the right. Release the tension on the leash instantly. The training collar will have tightened for an instant around the dog's neck and will then loosen. As you jerk the leash say "Cut" in a loud but not harsh tone of voice. Lavishly praise the dog immediately after the correction. You must not jerk the leash so as to cause pain. The desired effect is to startle or surprise the dog. Remember, "No" is said if you wish to eliminate barking altogether and "Cut" is said if you want to control the amount of barking the dog is allowed to do.

Do this every time he barks at noises, other dogs, strangers, or at anything. You can also correct a puppy with the use of a homemade noisemaker we call a *shake can* (see page 66 for details). When your dog barks, rattle the shake can behind your back vigorously, making a loud racket. Say "Cut" in a firm tone of voice and then praise him. A water gun or plant sprayer with water in it will also be effective in this instance.

When You Tie Your Puppy Up, He Barks and Howls

Never tie your dog up, no matter what. It is too restricting and could cause him to hurt himself. When you must confine your dog, keep him in a wire dog crate or in a room closed off with a see-through puppy gate. (See page 58 for more about confinement equipment.)

When Your Puppy Hears Noise, He Barks

When a dog barks at noise, he is behaving normally. Dogs have sensitive ears and they hear noises we don't. They will bark at sounds we may not even be aware of. The difference is between barking and *excessive* barking. If the dog barks too much when hearing noise, give him a leash correction or a shake-can correction, accompanied with the command CUT.

The Dog Seems to Bark for No Reason

There is almost always a reason why a dog barks. He hears noises, people, and other sounds you may not hear. Investigate the dog's environment and try to figure out why the dog is barking. It may be possible to eliminate the stimulus for the barking.

Your Dog Barks When You Leave Him Alone

The problem could stem from *how* you leave him alone. If you put your puppy in a room with the door closed, it could make him insecure and anxious. This will cause him to bark and howl. Depending on the age of the dog, leave him in the kitchen or laundry room with a see-through puppy gate or in a wire dog crate. (See page 58 for more about confinement equipment.)

Your Puppy Barks, and You Don't Know What He Wants

Puppies bark for many reasons. Maybe he's hungry, wants to play, needs exercise, or has to relieve himself. As babies have different kinds of crying sounds for various needs, puppies have different kinds of barking sounds for their various needs. Try to get in tune with your puppy's barks and what they may be trying to tell you. Create a checklist for the things your puppy may try to communicate to you by barking and refer to it as necessary.

When the Doorbell Rings, Your
Puppy Won't Stop Barking

The sound of the doorbell could affect your dog's hearing in some way and make him very uncomfortable. It could also intensify his instinct to guard his territory. If your dog will not stop barking after the doorbell rings, go to the door with him, give him a firm leash correction (or a shake-can correction). If you do this consistently, he will eventually stop this disturbing behavior.

Your Dog Barks All Night When
You Leave Him Outside

A dog will hear many sounds outdoors, such as other animals, people, and automobiles, that will set him off on long barking sessions. It is normal behavior for a dog. But ask yourself this: Why are you keeping your dog outside? Does he have a housebreaking problem? A chewing problem? Perhaps those are the problems that need attention. Keep your dog indoors and try to solve his other behavior problems.

First Week Home

Where to Keep Your Puppy the First Night

The best time to make this decision is before you bring the puppy home. The ideal place is a confined area with linoleum floor covering, such as the kitchen, the laundry room, the bathroom, or a hallway. The dog must be confined behind a see-through puppy gate, or in a wire dog crate where he can see out from all four sides. Make the area as comfortable as possible, with a blanket or dog bed, some chew toys, and a bowl of water. Keep the area lit with a subdued light, and turn on low-key music from the radio.

Your dog should be placed in the same area that you want

him to sleep in for the next few years. Do not create a situation that you will not like later on. If you allow the puppy to sleep with you on your bed, he will always expect to sleep there and that will always be a problem. Besides, puppies urinate through the night wherever they happen to be. They also squirm about restlessly, keeping you awake.

When and What to Feed Your Puppy

The first night in a new home is usually distressing for a puppy, and you should not add to his woes by giving him an upset stomach. You can avoid this by not changing his diet. Follow the feeding instructions from the breeder, shelter, or pet shop where you got the dog. Use the same food if possible, or an equivalent, and try to get at least a week's supply. Do not change anything until you have discussed the matter with your puppy's veterinarian.

A puppy under three months of age should be fed four times a day; from three months to six months, feed him three times a day; from six months to one year, feed him twice a day; and a dog over one year old should be fed only once a day. (See Chapters Seven and Eight for feeding schedules during paper training and housebreaking.)

What You Can Expect from Your Puppy

Your puppy is a small, vulnerable creature, entering an entirely new environment. At first he may be happy, outgoing, curious, and excited. But he will also become somewhat frightened, a little shy, and have several periods of anxiety (usually at night when the lights go out, for the first few nights). When he does, he will cry and howl. This is all normal.

What You Should Expect from Yourself

Your new puppy will need you to be patient, understanding, loving, and compassionate. Like a new mommy or daddy. It is very much like bringing a newborn baby home for the first time.

Unless you are made of stone, a new puppy will bring out your best parental instincts. Do not deny them or cover them up. Your feelings for the little dog will guide you.

What to Do When Your Puppy Cries All Night

Try to understand that the first few nights are going to be difficult for your new puppy. The change of environment is going to distress him. He may whine, whimper, cry, bark, or even howl. When he does, do not holler at him. This does not accomplish anything except to add to the little dog's stress. (To understand more about a brand-new puppy's behavior, refer to Chapter One.) A very young puppy that has just left his mother and littermates is going to miss the warmth, comfort, and security of being with them.

If you confine your puppy in a gated room or in a wire dog crate, it is important to get him used to being there long before bedding down for the night. Keeping your puppy energized with play and then suddenly placing him alone in a room for the night is too sudden a change. He is more than likely going to whine and howl. The puppy may not cry and carry on so much through the night if you confine him several times during the day and evening to help him adjust to the idea. Tucker him out with play an hour before bedtime and then let him slowly quiet down before confining him. This should help.

If your dog is placed in a wire dog crate, it is a good idea to place a large towel over the top and both sides to make it seem more like his very own den. Leave a dim light on, and perhaps a radio with soft music playing. Give the puppy a blanket or towel to curl up in. You could try placing a hot-water bottle wrapped in a towel next to him. The idea is to simulate the warmth of his mother's body. Some have even placed a ticking clock wrapped in a towel next to their dog to simulate the mother's heartbeat. Depending on your individual puppy, all of these things may or may not soothe the dog, but are well worth trying.

On one hand, you do not want to teach your dog that crying

will get him all the attention he wants. On the other hand, you will not "spoil" your puppy by going to him once or twice through the night and talking to him in a kind and gentle manner. Your dog's crying through the first two or three nights must be tolerated by all new dog owners. However, if your puppy continues to have a hard time longer than three or four nights you might try moving his crate into your bedroom for a few days. You must have faith that this condition will change once the dog adjusts to his new life.

The Puppy Has "Accidents"

All you can do is clean up your puppy's "accidents." Do not yell at the dog or say, "Bad dog." He is definitely going to soil the floor in these early days with you. See Chapter Seven and Eight for details about paper training and housebreaking your puppy. Be patient.

When to Start Saying "No" to Your Puppy

Give your dog at least a week with you before you begin using any kind of discipline. You wouldn't say "No" to a new baby, and you shouldn't do it right away with a puppy. The way to deal with your new puppy is to teach him what he can and cannot do. In the very beginning, be more patient and understanding and less concerned with discipline.

The Proper First-Night Attitude

You are bringing something new and wonderful into your life. But this creature is very young, vulnerable, and totally inexperienced about everything. This makes you something like a new parent and teacher. You will be responsible for showing this puppy what to do. What you do now will last for fifteen years. Think of your new dog as a foreigner in a strange land. How would you feel if you were in your dog's place? How would you treat a frightened child? Be patient, understanding, and compassionate.

The Great Escape

When You Open the Front Door, He Runs Out and Won't Come Back

This problem can only be solved by a closed door or through obedience training. (See Chapter Nine for more about training your puppy.) The command STAY is the proper command to prevent your dog from running out the door. If he doesn't run out in the first place, you won't have to worry about his coming back or not.

When the Gate Is Open, He Won't Stay

STAY is a precise obedience command that is usually taught in connection with the command SIT or DOWN. Merely telling your puppy to stay when you open the gate is meaningless. He must be taught the specifics of that command as part of an overall obedience course. To solve this problem, you must place an emphasis on teaching the command STAY. (See Chapter Nine for more about commands.)

When You Take Him Off the Leash, He Won't Come to You

If the dog has not been trained on-leash, there is no reason to expect him to obey your commands off-leash. (See Chapter Nine for more about training.) Another possible reason a dog does not come when called is lack of trust. If the dog was yelled at, or called "bad dog," or had his name used in a negative manner, then maybe he is uncertain about the reception he will get when he reaches you. You may discover that your behavior is the problem. Running to greet you when called should be your dog's happiest experience of the day, and if it isn't, then something is wrong with your relationship.

When He Sees Other Dogs. He Runs and Won't Listen to You

Only dogs that have been obedience trained can be relied upon to stay with you when other dogs are available. There is no reason for a dog to ignore his instinct to run with other dogs unless he has been taught the command STAY. (See Chapter Nine for more about commands.)

The Minute You Unsnap the Leash, the Dog Runs Away

Most dogs understand the difference between being on-leash and off-leash. When he hears that snap, he understands that he is free. Your only hope of preventing him from bolting away from you when you unleash him is if he is obedience trained (see Chapter Nine). To teach him not to bolt when you unsnap the leash, do this: Snap the spring clasp of the leash but do not take it off the collar. If the dog begins to bolt, give him a firm leash correction, say "No," and then praise him for obeying. Repeat this procedure until the dog no longer tries to run when you unsnap the leash.

Guilt

Your Dog Looks as if He Knows He's Done Something Wrong When You Come Home

Guilt is a *human* emotion and is not experienced by dogs. Dogs do not feel guilty or sorry for what they've done. When they get that woeful look, it is probably anxiety caused by anticipating your disapproval or punishment.

The typical scenario when the dog has done something wrong is for the owner to grab him and yell, "What did you do? Bad dog." This is usually accompanied by a pointed finger shaking at him. In some cases, the dog is hit, kicked, or chased out of the room. There are some who mistakenly believe it is effective to rub a dog's nose in his own mess after he has eliminated on the floor or carpet. The dog becomes frightened and very upset. He responds with that worried look because of the harsh sound of his owner's voice, threatening body language, and human manifestations of anger and disapproval.

After that experience the dog becomes anxious when his owner comes home, especially if he has repeated his "crime." If you didn't catch him in the act, he has *no idea* why he is being punished. That is why punishments are useless, and why canine guilt is never an issue. Behavior problems must be solved on the spot, with appropriate strategies and obedience training rather than angry reactions, especially after the fact. It never pays to make your puppy feel bad, because it does not teach anything. It can only alter your relationship with your dog.

You Feel Guilty When You Leave Your Dog Home Alone and Go to Work

You cannot quit your job. The bottom line is the quality of time you spend with your dog rather than the amount of time. Pay a lot of attention to your dog when you get up in the morning. Exercise him, walk him, play with him, feed him, talk to him, touch him. Maybe you can get someone to come to your house in the middle of the day to walk him. Do not give up your dog because you must work, and try not to feel guilty about it. At least the dog has a good home and someone who loves and cares for him.

You Feel Guilty When You Have to Board Your Dog

It is a fact that dogs do not feel bad in this situation. The owner is usually the one who feels bad about leaving. Although the dog is being placed temporarily in a different environment, he will probably enjoy the company of other dogs. What is most important is the quality of the boarding kennel. Will the kennel handlers be affectionate and give your dog the attention he needs? Will they provide good care? You should not give up your life and avoid traveling because of your dog. The best thing to do is find a *good* boarding kennel, where the people will care about your dog at least as much as you.

Jealousy

Your Dog Is Jealous of Your Child, Spouse, Lover, or Friend

In canine terms, jealousy could be defined as a set of expressed behaviors designed to compete for more attention. Although jealousy involves insecurity and competition, do not confuse human and canine emotions. Human jealousy is complex and involves anxiety, resentment, anger, and even hatred at times. When dogs are jealous they simply move closer to you in an obvious manner and try to get your attention. The issue for dogs is either attention, territory, or the order of rank in the "dog pack."

When children are present in the house, a jealous dog simply wants the same love and attention you give to your child. If there is a new baby in the house, some dogs feel replaced, neglected, or usurped from their order of rank. In addition, they may actually be upset by the new sounds, smells, and rearrangement of the household. Rarely does a dog behave in a dangerous manner when it is jealous. However, just to be on the safe side, it is always best to supervise all contact between a baby and a dog and *never* leave them alone together.

When a puppy (or a grown dog) behaves in a jealous manner, the solution is easy and direct: Reassure him with added attention and expressions of affection. This should be done at a time when the object of the dog's competition is not around. Otherwise, you will always be in the position of having to pet the dog whenever you deal with your child. As with a firstborn child, give your dog what he needs, but only when it is reasonable. When your dog's jealous behavior is annoying or aggressive, you can use a leash correction or a voice correction to stop it (see Chapter Nine).

Your Dog Becomes Jealous When You Pay Attention to Your Other Dog(s)

If one dog nuzzles in for petting whenever you are petting another dog, it isn't really jealousy. It is a desire for your affection, since you're giving it out. The problem is solved if you think of all your dogs' needs and desires at the same time. See "Your Dog Is Jealous of Your Child . . ." for more information.

You Are Jealous. Your Dog Obeys Someone Else More Readily Than He Obeys You

Each person who knows the dog may have a different relationship with him, and you should enjoy it for what it is. If you want your dog to obey you more than he does, you must assume a more dominant role in your relationship with him. You must be more like a pack leader. If you want him to listen to you in a positive way, then you must be instrumental in his care and training.

Jumping on Furniture

How to Stop Your Dog from Jumping on the Furniture

If jumping on furniture is behavior you want to stop, then use the correction/praise technique described in Chapter Nine. It requires use of a training collar and leash. Place them on the puppy and leave the room. The idea is to catch the dog in the act. If you see him jump on the furniture, run into the room, grab the leash, and jerk it to your right side, giving the dog a mild, negative sensation. As you do this, say "No" in a firm tone of voice. Guide the dog off the furniture with the leash and praise him lavishly as you do. It is important that you immediately follow the correction with enthusiastic praise, such as

"Good dog." That is the teaching portion of the technique and is as important as the correction itself.

You can also correct a puppy with the use of a homemade noisemaker we call a shake can. See page 66 for details. When you catch your dog on the furniture, rattle the shake can behind your back vigorously, making a loud racket. Say "No" in a very firm tone of voice. This will startle the dog and make him hop off the sofa. As he does this, praise him. A water gun or plant sprayer filled with water will also be effective when used in this instance.

How to Stop the Dog from Jumping on the Furniture When You're Not Home

Try to create in your dog an aversion to the furniture. The idea is to have him develop an unpleasant association with the furniture so that he won't want to jump on it. The following techniques are safe and not the least bit harmful.

Balloons Go to the puppy and sit on the floor next to him. Do not call him to you, because you never want to call him to you for something unpleasant. Slowly and with great ceremony (so that you capture his interest) blow up a balloon to its full size. Let him look at it, sniff it, and even touch it. Without warning, stick it with a pin so that it will explode with a loud pop. It should startle the dog. Repeat this action. Next, blow up five or ten balloons and tie them off. Tape them to the piece of furniture you suspect the dog is jumping on when you're not home. Leave the house. The dog is likely to associate the balloons with the unpleasant explosion that just startled him and stay away from them. For one week repeat this every time you leave the house. Do not use this technique if your dog is shy. (See Chapter Three to determine your dog's personality type.)

Mousetraps If the balloon technique does not get results, or if your dog is a hard case, buy four or five mousetraps at a hardware store. Place them on the furniture the dog jumps on and set them. *We do not want you to hurt the dog, so please cover the* *mousetraps with several sheets of newspaper.* Tape the papers down so they won't blow away and endanger the dog by exposing the traps. The traps will snap loudly when the puppy jumps on the papers and will scare him. We predict he will jump off the furniture and stay away from it. Repeat this for one week.

Aluminum Foil If your dog is not a hard case, you can try creating a sensory aversion to the furniture he loves to jump on. Tape several long, single sheets of aluminum foil to completely cover the cushions or pillows of the furniture. The sight, sound, and slippery feeling beneath his paws will make the furniture undesirable to him. Do this for one week.

Small Puppy on Your Lap

Allowing your puppy to sit on your lap while you are seated on the furniture is the same as teaching him to jump on the furniture. It could eventually lead to dirty or destroyed furniture. If you do not want your puppy to grow up to be a dog that jumps on your furniture, then you must not allow him on your lap while you are sitting on the couch or in a chair. It is a choice that must be made.

Small Puppy on Your Bed

Allowing your puppy on your bed is the same as teaching him to jump on your furniture. He will not be able to make the distinction between the bed and other pieces of furniture. Many dogs that are allowed on furniture end up chewing it, scratching it, dirtying it, and sometimes infesting it with fleas. You must decide whether your puppy is allowed on your furniture or not. If he is not, then you must also keep him off the bed.

Occasionally a puppy will not jump on the furniture even if he is allowed on the bed. This may be acceptable to you when he is a puppy but not such a good idea when he grows into an adult dog. There is a world of difference between a German Shepherd puppy and a full-grown adult of that breed. Will you want a canine bed partner that weighs sixty, eighty, or ninety pounds?

Also, there is no guarantee that a puppy or adult dog will not behave destructively on your bed or perhaps scent mark it with his urine or stool.

Small Puppy Sleeping with Your Child

This is a pleasant fantasy of most parents and their children. However, there may be consequences for permitting this. Some dogs claim a bed as their personal territory once they are allowed to sleep in it, which can result in scent marking it with urine and stool or actually fighting for it. It is also an invitation to the dog to sleep on furniture all over your house. We do not recommend that puppies or dogs be allowed to sleep in a child's bed.

Giving Your Puppy an Old Chair or Sofa of His Own

This is fine providing the dog stays on his own piece of furniture. If the dog takes it into his head to move to your furniture, you are going to have a problem and will have to introduce the various correction and aversion techniques described earlier. While your dog is still a puppy, you have an opportunity to prevent this problem from developing by never allowing him on the furniture in the first place.

Jumping on People

How to Stop the Problem Before It Starts

We teach our puppies to jump on us and on others by lifting them to our laps in response to their jumping on our legs. It is an unintentional reward for doing the wrong thing. When you allow your dog to sit in your lap too many times or for too long a time or whenever he is excited, you are not only teaching him to jump on you (and others) but also to sit on the furniture.

To prevent this, sit on the floor when holding the puppy. You may then allow him to crawl and climb on you. He then begins to associate jumping on you with your being on the floor. You must be consistent. It is not logical to expect a dog to be allowed to jump on you as a puppy but not later on when he has grown to full size.

Jumping on You and No One Else

We all want to express our love and affection for a puppy and we also want to experience the puppy's feelings for us. Because of this we see no harm in allowing the little dog to jump on us. But it is not reasonable to expect a dog to understand being allowed to jump on you, but not on anyone else. Consistency is the most important aspect of clearing up this problem. You must decide if the dog is allowed to jump on people or not. If you do not want the dog to jump on other people, then do not allow him to jump on you, not even as a puppy.

New dog owners cannot see the harm in allowing a little puppy to jump on them. It becomes a problem if the dog is fully grown and can injure them, or if they are dressed in their best clothes and do not want to be smudged with dirt, saliva, or dog fur. You may not mind if you live with a little Yorkie, but when a full-grown Old English Sheepdog jumps on you in your dress clothes, you might feel differently.

How to Stop Your Dog from Jumping on People

If you consider jumping on people undesirable behavior, then consistently discourage the practice by correcting the dog each and every time he attempts to do it. The most effective corrections are accomplished with a leash and a training collar. To learn how to correct your puppy with this technique, see Chapter Nine. It requires that you put the leash and collar on the dog and let him wear them all day. When he attempts to jump on you, jerk the leash to the side and to your left, giving the dog a mild, negative sensation. As you do this say "No" in a firm tone of voice. The dog has no choice but to get off you. It is important that you immediately follow the correction with enthusiastic praise, such as "Good dog." The praise is as important as the correction itself if the dog is going to learn properly.

You can also correct a puppy with the use of a homemade noisemaker we call a shake can. (See page 66 for details.) Place several strategically around your home, including one near the front door. When you walk in, have the shake can behind your back. When the dog jumps on you shake it vigorously, making a loud racket. Say "No" in a very firm tone of voice. This will startle the dog and make him stop jumping on you. Praise the dog the instant he gets off your leg. A water gun or plant sprayer filled with water will also be effective for correcting a dog.

Do Not Knee Your Dog in the Chest to Solve This Problem

The old technique of knocking a dog off you by kneeing him in the chest is not at all acceptable. It is a very harsh thing to do and does not teach the dog anything except fear of you. You must never use your body in a negative manner with your dog; this tears at the bond that you have so carefully created between you and serves to interfere with training.

Kneeing a dog can hurt him. Most of the time the knee misses the chest and catches him in the legs, the neck, or the face. If you are going to solve this problem, use the correction and praise methods described above.

Leaving the Puppy Home

You Feel Guilty When You Go to Work and Leave the Puppy Alone

You cannot give up your job for your puppy. Although the puppy may at times become bored, he does not feel bad. You are the one feeling bad. As long as the dog is confined properly so that he cannot get into trouble, has water, toys, and is being properly housebroken or paper trained, he will be fine. There is no reason to feel guilty.

Where to Keep Your Puppy When You're Gone All Day

A house with a fenced-in yard is fine (weather permitting), and so is an outdoor dog run. Inside the home, the laundry room, the kitchen, or a spacious hallway are all suitable areas, provided the dog can be confined with a see-through puppy gate. Do not place your dog, *no matter what his age,* in a room with a closed door. It is important for him to be able to see another part of the house from his area of confinement. A dog crate is useful for periods of confinement of four hours or less, but not for the entire day. That would be harmful and unkind. (For more details about confining your dog, see page 58.)

When You Leave Him Alone, You're Worried He Will Destroy Everything

This is an important consideration, and the answer is to avoid giving a puppy (or a new dog) the run of the house. A puppy could be destructive until he's two years old (or longer), and you must place him in an area that is puppy-proof. A hallway, bathroom, kitchen, or a fenced-in yard or outdoor dog run (weather permitting) are suitable for this purpose. All you need is an appropriate method for confining the dog such as a see-through puppy gate or a dog crate. (For more about confinement equipment, see page 58.)

When You Come Home, the Entire Yard Is Full of Holes

Your dog has a digging problem. Dogs have an instinct to create a den for themselves and consequently dig into soft ground, lawns, snow, sand, or anything they can sink their paws into.

There are various methods of "self-correcting" this problem. If the dog returns to the same spot to dig, as is often the case, place a large rock in the hole and cover it up with dirt. You can also fill the hole with a large quantity of aluminum foil, chicken wire, gravel, crushed pebbles, or combinations of these things. You can even place a large, inflated balloon in the hole. Then cover it up with the original dirt. The idea is to make digging that hole as unpleasant as possible.

When You Come Home, Your Neighbors Tell You He Wouldn't Stop Crying

Ask your neighbors when the dog was crying, under what circumstances he was crying, and where he was at the time. The answers to those questions will help you find the solution to the problem.

When You Come Home, You Find Housebreaking Accidents in the House

Do not get angry at the puppy because he has housebreaking accidents. When a puppy is not yet housebroken, or is only partially housebroken, he should not have the run of the entire house. The dog must be confined to one area with the help of a see-through puppy gate or a dog crate. (Never confine a dog to a crate for more than four hours, two or three for a puppy.) If your puppy is very young, he will not be able to control himself at this time, which means he must be walked more frequently to allow him to eliminate. You must weigh the dog's age against the housebreaking schedule he is on. (See Chapters Seven and Eight for more about paper training and housebreaking.)

When You Come Home, You Find Him Sleeping on Your Bed

The dog should not have access to your bed. The dog should be confined in a room that has no bed or furniture in it. Wherever you confine the dog, make him comfortable with a dog bed of his own, a blanket, a towel, or even a carpet remnant.

When You Come Home and Find That He Did Something Wrong, He Will Not Come to You

This is always the result when inexperienced dog owners yell at their dogs for misbehaving. Punishing the dog for his misbehavior or even yelling "Bad dog" makes the animal nervous about approaching you. No dog is going to be happy to run to someone who is going to yell at him. We believe you cannot correct a dog unless you catch him in the act.

What to Do When You Cannot Be at Home All Day to Take Him Out

If you do not have a fenced-in yard, you will have to hire a dog walker or ask a neighbor, friend, or relative to take the dog out in the middle of the day. Young dogs, especially those being housebroken, *must* have a midday walk to relieve themselves and get a bit of exercise.

The Best Place to Keep Your Puppy When You're Not Home All Day

Ideally, the best places are areas that can be made puppy-proof, such as the kitchen, the laundry room, a long hallway, even a bathroom, providing the area is closed off with a see-through puppy gate. If the weather permits, a fenced-in yard or dog run is also suitable. Never keep a dog in a dog crate for more than four hours, two or three for a puppy.

Nipping and Biting

When You Try to Pet Him, He Bites You Playfully

All puppies use their mouths as a form of communication. Hunger, pain, and pleasure are but a few of the feelings expressed by biting. Also, many puppies teethe and gnaw on anything handy to help ease their pain and discomfort.

To stop this behavior and to prevent it from becoming a permanent habit, place a leash and training collar on your puppy when playing with him. When he nips at any part of you, give him an appropriate leash correction (based on his personality). Say "No" in a firm tone of voice. Tell him he's a good dog immediately afterward. (See Chapter Nine for more about training.)

When You Hold Him, He Tries to Bite You All Over

When a puppy is teething he is going to bite and nip at the closest thing available, and your body is by all means fair game. For this reason it is recommended that you refrain from holding the little dog until this stage of behavior has passed. (Puppies usually finish teething by their sixth month.) Do not offer him your finger to nip on. It may be cute now but can create permanent aggressive behavior.

Your Puppy Won't Stop Biting Your Legs and Pants

As you walk, your puppy sees all this wonderful flapping material, close to his mouth. As far as he's concerned this is great, because biting on just about anything—including your legs and pants—feels good.

You can alleviate the problem by giving the little dog an appropriate substitute for your lower extremities. Whenever your puppy nips at your feet or legs, say "No" in a firm tone of voice and praise him for stopping. Then offer him something that will satisfy his teething needs without creating negative behavior problems. Chew toys or ice-cold washcloths will suffice. However, do not give him any food, such as dog biscuits. That will only reward him for biting and reinforce the behavior.

When Puppies Stop Biting

Normal nipping and biting behavior usually ends by six months of age. This behavior can and should be stopped sooner by using leash and collar corrections (see Chapter Nine for more about corrections) in conjunction with firm voice commands, or the methods described earlier under "Eventually Puppies Stop Chewing," page 80.

When You Play Tug-of-War with Him, He Won't Stop

Games of this sort are fun for most puppies. They will not stop until they get tired. Such games encourage aggressive behavior that lasts for a lifetime. Playing tug-of-war with some puppies is like teaching them to be aggressive or even teaching them to bite. It is important to avoid playing such games. They offer no benefit for you or your dog. Playing fetch is just as effective and far less provocative.

When You Play with Him with Your Hands on His Face, He Tries to Bite You

It is a predictable result, because the problem is created by the play itself. Placing your hands on a dog's face with vigor is an aggressive action, and even a puppy is stimulated in a negative way. Like tug-of-war, it is the type of play that is best avoided. A game such as retrieving a stick, a ball, or a Frisbee is just as much fun and does no harm to the dog's character.

Spite/Anger

You Think Your Dog Is Spiteful Because He Chews When You're Not Home

Dogs chew when no one is home because they are either bored, anxious, or have separation anxiety. Spite is a human emotion that involves malice and ill will and can take many forms and vary in degrees of intensity. Spite can be expressed as stubborn resistance or as violence. Often spite is expressed in terms of revenge, and it is hard to believe that dogs exhibit such behavior. There is no evidence that dogs are capable of experiencing such a complex set of thoughts and emotions. Dogs are basically simple. Although there are some similarities, dog behavior is unique and quite different from human behavior. If your dog chews destructively when you are not home, he has a chewing problem, not a spite problem. Refer to "Chewing" in this chapter.

You Think Your Dog Is Spiteful Because He Wets in Front of You

This is simply not true. Spite has nothing to do with this problem. The reasons for uncontrollable wetting are drinking too much water, fear of punishment, fear of people, excitability, nervousness, illness, poor housebreaking, or because the dog is not walked often enough. Your options are to see a veterinarian, reduce the dog's water intake, and take care not to overexcite your dog. Greet your excitable dog in the yard or on the porch to avoid pee on the floor. Do not intimidate a shy dog with overbearing behavior or body language. (See Chapter Three to determine your dog's personality type.) Kneel down to eye level and never holler, threaten, or hit him.

You Think Your Dog Is Spiteful Because He Barks and Cries Only When You Leave

Dogs are not spiteful. They may bark and cry because they miss you, because you are confining them improperly, because they are hungry. They may bark and cry because of a new and drastic change in your daily schedule. Too much affection and attention given to the dog just before leaving will cause excessive barking. Do not think of this behavior as spiteful. Refer to "Excessive Barking" in this chapter.

Yard Problems

When You Leave Your Puppy in the Yard, He Digs Holes Everywhere and Chews All Your Flowers and Plants

If your dog is a very young puppy, this behavior is normal. Confine the little dog in one small area of your yard within a wire pen enclosure designed for small dogs, or devise some type of dog run, and as he matures, increase the space in which he has to play.

When You're Not Home, the Dog Jumps Over the Fence

Your fence must be puppy-proof. Typically, this means it must be at least six feet or higher to be effective. Some dogs can actually climb over a fence, depending on the type of fence you have. Maybe there is a step or a ledge that helps him get over. You must evaluate your fence and remedy the situation if necessary.

Your Puppy Chews All the Cushions on Your Lawn Chairs

Remove the cushions. You can purchase alum powder from a pharmacy and mix it with a bit of water into a spreadable paste. Spread it on the part of the cushions the dog loves to chew. The mixture is unpleasant to the taste and causes an unpleasant, puckering sensation in the dog's mouth. He will never return to the scene of the crime after tasting the mixture.

Your Dog Jumps into the Pool When You're Not Home

Would you permit a child to use a swimming pool without adult supervision? The same should apply to young dogs. You need to determine if your dog can swim instinctively to save himself in case he accidentally gets into the pool. Being able to swim is by no means enough. He must be able to get out of the pool without your help. Some dogs have to be taught how to get out, and must be shown where the pool steps are. A puppy could easily drown if he were to get into a swimming pool when no one was there to rescue him. If you are not home, you must take every precaution to prevent your puppy from having access to the pool.

SEVEN

HOUSEBREAKING YOUR PUPPY

When it comes to housebreaking a puppy, an ounce of prevention is worth a pound of cure . . . or perhaps *pounds* of cure. Dogs are not like us; they have an entirely different view of their body waste. Dogs beam with pride at the sight of their own stools. A dog's waste products reek of his personal odor and give him the same sense of identity that we experience from our creative accomplishments. A dog's urine and feces mean a great deal to him: The scent allows him to identify where he and other dogs have been, to claim territory, to find partners for mating, to declare his rank in the social order, to express satisfaction, and to express his anxiety. So you see, there is more to this than meets the eye, or nose, as the case may be.

The most difficult problem owners of new puppies face is getting their little dog to eliminate his body waste in a place acceptable to the owners. Few pet owners can tolerate dog stools and urine all over the floor. If this problem is not solved quickly and effectively, the puppy's status in his new home is in jeopardy. Housebreaking a puppy can be a frustrating, confusing process when you do not understand what is going on or how to proceed properly. It is a matter of understanding why the dog behaves the way he does, how he uses his own instincts to fit in with your needs, how you can communicate your instructions, and what housebreaking really is.

Housebreaking, by Definition

Housebreaking means your puppy is trained to pee and poop *outdoors*, on a schedule you determine. He must always control himself until he can be taken out. Once the dog has been trained to do this he must never relieve himself indoors.

Housebreaking and Paper Training Are Not the Same Thing

It is important that you do not confuse paper training with housebreaking. Paper training and housebreaking involve methods that are somewhat similar but have significant differences. These two methods of training represent different lifestyles for dogs, and each has its own demands and requirements. Only housebreaking will be discussed in this chapter. For a more complete understanding of the distinction, we suggest that you also read Chapter Eight, on paper training.

The most common mistake puppy owners make is using newspapers on the floor as a temporary measure until the little dog is able to do his business outdoors. Sometimes the puppy is encouraged to use newspapers on the floor *and* the great outdoors. This tends to drag out the housebreaking process without success because it confuses the dog.

Why You Should Choose One or the Other

When dogs relieve themselves, there are several objectives involved besides the elimination of body waste. Males (and some females) mark the boundaries of their territory with urine or feces, which explains why they prefer one or more specific places to relieve themselves. Although territory is almost always at issue, some dogs are much more territorial than others. Other objectives are declaring sexual availability (females, especially those in heat, give off a special odor that is attractive to males), announcing dominance over other dogs in the area, or challenging others' dominance.

Despite what you may have heard, you must not paper train your puppy as a first step to housebreaking. The reason is simple: When you introduce newspapers for toileting purposes you are teaching your puppy to relieve himself on the floor in addition to helping him establish territory and assert himself through the messages sent by his odor. He will then continually return to the same locations that have his scent on them and relieve himself on top of the original odor *whether there is paper there or not.* If you have ever watched a dog taken out for his walk, you may have seen him search for a specific location with his nose to the ground and then finally pee once he finds it. He has sniffed out his or another dog's odor and then marked it with his urine or feces. This is called *scent posting* and is an important instinctive behavior for all dogs. It cannot, nor should it, be stopped. However, you can manipulate this instinct to your advantage. You can obliterate the unacceptable location of a scent post and help your dog establish one at a location more acceptable to you.

By spreading out newspapers on the floor you teach your puppy to claim (and constantly reclaim) territory in your home by scent posting. Some puppies grow up without the ability or the inclination to control this behavior and develop the habit of scent posting many parts of your home. It is difficult for some puppies to confine their eliminating behavior to one area of the house after they have been given newspapers to use on the floor. After all, they have been taught to do this.

From a behavioral point of view, it is a mistake to use newspapers on the floor as a *temporary* measure before teaching your puppy to go outdoors. *The worst situation for a puppy is to be given newspapers to use on the floor for a week or two and then have them suddenly taken away. Then the dog gets hollered at and punished for continuing to use the floor (without the papers) simply because his family now wants him to go outdoors.* There is no logic or justice in this for the puppy. There is only confusion.

Another reason you should not use newspapers as a temporary measure is the issue of *surface*. A puppy that has been given newspapers to pee on may have a more difficult time learning to go outdoors than one that is housebroken from the start. Part of the problem lies with the surface the dog scrapes his feet on after relieving himself. In nature, wild dogs and wolves urinate and defecate as part of the scent-posting process. But another form of marking territory that often accompanies scent posting is leaving a visual mark. Many dogs scratch the ground with their front or rear paws after eliminating to offer further evidence of their presence in the area. It looks as if they are wiping their feet.

This behavior is very important to the dogs that do it. Some puppies find it impossible to relieve themselves on a surface that is different from the one they were first introduced to. Puppies that were taught to *temporarily* relieve themselves on newspapers may have trouble adjusting to the surface of a street or even a yard without paper under their paws. Consequently, some dog owners find themselves in the ridiculous position of having to lay out sheets of newspapers on the street so that their dogs will go.

Many veterinarians suggest that a newly acquired puppy should not be taken outdoors for a specific period of time because the animal does not have sufficient immunities against

disease built up in his body. If this situation applies to you and
your puppy, and you have decided that the dog is to be housebroken, here is a suggestion: *Do not attempt to paper train the dog.*
Select an area that is convenient for you and the puppy and
place several sheets of newspaper there. When the puppy is
about to eliminate, place him on the papers but do not scold
him or correct him in any way. The same applies if he has an accident off the papers. Although it is a nuisance, you will be rewarded for your patience once the housebreaking begins. When
the veterinarian says the puppy is allowed outdoors, the newspapers should be removed completely and all sites thoroughly
cleaned with a cleaning product specially designed to neutralize
the scent (see page 132.) You may now begin using the housebreaking methods outlined in the remainder of this chapter. If
you do this, you will not confuse your puppy.

The best situation is to begin housebreaking your puppy the
minute he comes to live with you. But if this conflicts with instructions from your veterinarian, who advises you to keep your
young dog indoors until his immunity against disease is assured,
we do not suggest that you ignore your veterinarian's advice. However, you must understand that allowing your puppy to relieve
himself on newspapers and then getting him to go outdoors,
without soiling in your house, causes behavioral confusion. The
changeover will take longer and demand greater effort and patience on your part.

How to Housebreak Your Puppy

This method works well for puppies and dogs between the ages
of seven weeks and three years, although it has been effective for
many dogs as old as twelve years of age. Even though a young
puppy will be more responsive to training than an older dog,
contrary to popular belief, there is no rule that says you can't
teach an old dog new tricks. It will take longer to housebreak an

older dog, but the method will work if the owner adheres to all the techniques suggested here.

The ideal time to housebreak a puppy is as soon as he is brought into your home. Start the training as soon as your veterinarian has given your puppy all of his required inoculations and has given you the go-ahead to take him outdoors.

Some puppies are easy to housebreak and learn what you want quickly, but not all puppies are alike. Some take much longer than others. The housebreaking training period may last three days, ten days, three weeks, or even longer, depending on the dog and how effectively you use these techniques. No matter what the circumstances, you should notice significant progress by the end of the first week of training. If there is no progress by the second week, it is possible that the animal is not well and should be taken to a veterinarian. If a dog has worms, as many puppies do, he will not be able to control his digestive system, and housebreaking becomes impossible until the condition is corrected.

The techniques for housebreaking are based on six easy elements: (1) Proper diet, (2) Confinement to one area, (3) Selecting a good outdoor location, (4) Correction, (5) Appropriate feeding and walking schedule, and (6) Getting rid of the scent-posting odor. Assuming your puppy is allowed outdoors and is in good health, these six elements should be carefully observed.

Proper Diet

How and what you feed your puppy have an important influence on his mind and body. The proper balance of vitamins, minerals, proteins, carbohydrates, fats, and electrolytes (found in water) is essential to the growth and development of a puppy. An intelligent and consistent diet is of great importance, and this is especially true while training.

Coping with Stress Training can be stressful, and stress makes greater nutritional demands on the canine body. The relationship between proper diet and housebreaking is notably important if you consider that you are teaching your dog how to control his need to eliminate. On one hand, you do not want to disrupt your dog's digestive system, especially when you are housebreaking him. On the other, you may want to adjust his diet if he becomes stressed at this time.

Stress can be caused by an added or unusual physical or emotional demand made on the body. The body then responds with a stress reaction, which causes the internal systems to mobilize. The heartbeat and breathing rate increase, and the muscles begin to tense. This creates a demand for extra energy. Protein is taken from tissue reserves and other sources and used to manufacture glucose, antibodies, and new blood cells. This may require a food higher in protein or simply a bit more of the ration currently being fed. Visible signs of stress may be appetite loss, bad behavior, apathy, or depression.

If your puppy becomes stressed, it may not necessarily be caused by training. Stress is often caused by internal or external parasites, bacteria or viruses, strenuous physical activity, anxiety, or emotional upset. A lack of attention or affection, for example, could create a stress response. You may prevent stress by improving your puppy's diet, keeping him in good spirits with needed attention and play, and by lavishing him with affection, especially during the training period.

Selecting the Right Dog Food All the essentials of sound nutrition can be found in most of the premium dog foods that are available in grocery stores, supermarkets, and pet-supply stores. Some dog foods can even be purchased from your veterinarian. Dog food comes in various forms, including dry, canned, and semimoist. There are many commercial dog foods, but choose one with a label indicating that it meets the daily minimum requirements for dogs (as established by the National Research Council's Committee on Animal Nutrition).

A premium dog food will probably meet your pet's nutritional requirements. But it is best to select a food that is formulated for your puppy's age range. Examine the label of the dog food and make sure it says "complete and balanced," or words to that effect. Every dog is different. If there is the slightest doubt about what to feed your dog, we suggest you consult your veterinarian.

When housebreaking a puppy it is essential that you get him on a diet that is appropriate for his age and lifestyle. This, of course, is essential for his proper rate of growth and development but also to aid the training process. Your dog should not be fed a diet of leftovers from your dinner table, especially while he is being housebroken. A dinner of leftovers, no matter how large a quantity, does not guarantee that the dog is getting all the nutrition he needs. Also, feeding a dog from the table actually teaches him the annoying habit of begging for food. Most important of all, it does not work well with the feeding schedule that is such an important part of this training method. Inadequate diet, irregular feeding times, snacks between meals, and sudden changes of food all work against the training. If your puppy develops digestion problems, such as diarrhea, during the training process, it will not work. It is important that you feed your dog properly if the housebreaking process is to be successful.

Confinement to One Area

Do not give your puppy the run of the house until you are satisfied that he is completely housebroken. Accidents on the floor require corrections, and too many accidents and corrections may delay the success of the program. During the housebreaking period, the puppy must always be watched so that he can be corrected in the middle of an accident. If you are too busy to watch the dog, or if you must leave the house, it is essential that you confine him to the area you have established for that purpose.

A Puppy's Desire to Keep His Nest Clean Most puppies will try to avoid soiling in an area that is close to where they must eat and sleep. This behavior may be instinctive but is probably learned from the mother. For the first three weeks of life, the mother tends to the puppies' need to eliminate and keeps the nest clean. After that, she does not tolerate soiling in the nest. Thereafter, it is the puppy's inclination to soil as far away from his nest as possible. However, far too many puppies are removed from the litter before this behavior takes hold. This is particularly true of dogs from puppy mills and some pet shops. Such dogs will soil their own eating and sleeping area. They simply have not been taught otherwise.

Self-Control A puppy does not have a great deal of muscular control over urinating and defecating and will relieve himself wherever he happens to be at the time of his need. If he is confined where he eats and sleeps, he may control himself while you are away. If there is enough room, he will at least attempt to relieve himself as far away from his bed, food, and water as possible. This will help teach him to control his body and wait until you are there to take him out.

Where to Confine Your Puppy It is essential that you establish an area where you can confine the puppy. The most convenient location is the kitchen, where the floor is probably covered with linoleum or some other moisture-proof material. The area of confinement should be large enough so your dog does not feel he is being punished when placed there. It should not be closed off by a solid door. If the area is too small or the doorway is blocked off, the puppy will whine, howl, or bark excessively, and you will come home to angry neighbors. Install a see-through puppy gate (see Chapter Four, page 58). Do not use a folding gate for a small dog. Small puppies are capable of crawling under the bottom and getting loose in the house when you are not home. Never tie your dog down with a rope, chain, or leash when you leave the house. This will have an adverse effect on your puppy's personality and work against the training.

The area of confinement may be a wire dog crate conveniently placed where the puppy can see what's going on around him (see Chapter Four). If you decide to use a dog crate, it is important to remember that a puppy should not remain in it for

longer than two or three hours at a time. A mature dog can remain for a longer period—up to four hours—but never for an
entire day. Use the wire dog crate as you would any other area of
confinement as detailed in this chapter.

How to Use the Confinement Area as a Training Method

Every time you return home, allow your puppy to leave the
confined area, clean up after him if he soiled his area (do not
holler at him or punish him), and make your return pleasurable
for both you and the puppy. Allow him to run loose in the
house, and watch him carefully for accidents. Do not punish
him if he messes on the floor, but correct him if you catch him
in the act. If he gets out of your sight and makes a mistake, there
is nothing you can do but clean it up and return him to his area
of confinement.

Selecting a Good Outdoor Location

New puppy owners who have a backyard will undoubtedly
want to use it as a place for their little dog to relieve himself.
And that's fine providing you understand how unappealing that
may be once the puppy matures into a grown dog—large dogs
leave large deposits. If you do not maintain a high degree of san-
itation and hygiene, you will not only create an eyesore for you
and your neighbors, you may also create an unhealthy environment. When not cleaned up quickly, feces and urine can leave
behind bacteria, viruses, fungi, and all manner of parasites, including worms and fleas. You may want to rethink your position
on using the backyard.

If you live in the city or suburbs, it is best to allow your dog
to use the streets as a place to relieve himself, but under certain
conditions. Many communities have "scoop" laws that require
dog owners to clean up after their dogs. This is not as awful a
task as it sounds. There is a wide variety of gadgets for sale to
help you accomplish the job, and for the less squeamish, plastic

bags, paper towels, or newspapers will do just fine. Dog owners who are good neighbors and sensitive to the requirements of non–dog owners help prevent antidog legislation from getting started in their own communities.

Earlier in this chapter you were informed of your dog's instinct to scent post various locations with his urine and feces as a method of declaring himself in the area. It involves the drive to claim territory, to establish his dominance, and possibly to assist in the mating process. Where the dog first eliminates will be a place that he will return to, time and time again. Why not choose that location yourself rather than allow the dog to make the choice? Select an area that is convenient, safe, and not upsetting to your neighbors.

If you will be coming home with a new puppy soon, then you have an opportunity to make the scent-posting choices for your dog. Whether coming home from a kennel, a shelter, or a pet shop, your puppy will want to relieve himself the minute he steps out of the car. Do not go directly into your house. Walk to the outdoor place that is going to be the toilet area and place the small dog on the ground. This first action begins the dog's housebreaking and goes far to make the training easier. Give the puppy at least ten minutes to eliminate, and once he does, shower him with loving praise. Pet the dog and tell him what a great thing he has accomplished and point to the evidence as you offer your congratulations. Allow the puppy to sniff at his great achievement so he can associate your praise with his own accomplishment. From that time on, always return to the same spot with the puppy, whenever he is taken out to relieve himself. In the beginning, it is a good idea to carry him there so that he does not scent post another location that is not desirable.

Correction

Among the many misconceptions of dog training, hitting the dog to teach him is the greatest. It is a mistake to think that the dog has learned something by being hit or yelled at or by having his nose rubbed in his own mess. The underlying philosophy of this housebreaking method is simply that *correction* must be used instead of *punishment.*

You can correct your puppy only when you witness his mistake. His ability to understand your anger or your punishment is very limited. Therefore, a dog cannot associate a smack on the rump with a mess on the floor if he transgressed before you arrived on the scene. Even a few minutes after he messed is enough time to make him stare dumbfounded and wonder why you are hollering. Punishment, even proper correction, affects very little after the fact. Spare yourself the energy and the dog the confusion. Correct the animal only when you catch him in the middle of his mistake.

How to Correct Your Dog Assuming the dog is peeing or pooping indoors during the period of housebreaking and is doing it in front of you, there is only one way to respond. You must startle the puppy so that he stops what he is doing and then rush him outside to finish.

Do not holler, hit, or threaten him. Do not use a rolled-up newspaper or even an admonishing pointed finger to express your dissatisfaction. All you will do is frighten your dog. Fear is not the basis for a loving relationship or for sound teaching. Instead, you must communicate to your puppy that he did the wrong thing. This is accomplished with a *correction.* A correction could be one of several communicating techniques. All corrections must be followed immediately with verbal praise so that the puppy feels rewarded for having stopped his misbehavior. It also tells him that you are not mad at him. Puppies should be stopped in the middle of making a mistake with a verbal correction and a noise correction *only.* If you catch your little dog in the middle of a soiling mistake, say "No" in a firm tone of voice. At the same time vigorously rattle a shake can (see Chapter Four). Because shake cans cost nothing to make, you should have several placed in convenient locations around your home. Do not point your finger at the dog as if to say, "Naughty, naughty." Your hands should be used only for positive actions and gestures.

Here is how to correct your puppy when he relieves himself on the floor: Say "No" in a very firm tone of voice. Reach for a shake can and rattle it, making a loud noise. This will startle the dog and possibly get him to stop relieving himself. Scoop him up in your hands, put his leash and collar on, and carry him outside to finish his business there. Once he does, lavish him with praise. This is the teaching aspect of correction. You have stopped the puppy from going in the wrong place and shown him where going is desirable. The correction told him his action was wrong. The praise for going on the street told him his action was right. All dogs want to please the leader of their pack and they will begin to work for your praise by doing the right thing. All that is necessary is for you to correct your puppy when he does the wrong thing and praise him when he does the right thing.

It is essential that you consider your dog's personality when correcting him. If the noise from the shake can is too loud or "No" is said too harshly, you could alter his personality in a negative way or damage your relationship with him. Never use the shake can with a shy or timid puppy, or one that is shy combined with a high-energy personality. (See Chapter Three to determine your dog's personality type.) Do not use the shake can with any dog that cowers in fear of it.

A shy dog or a shy/high-energy dog requires a soft tone of voice when saying "No" and no noise corrections from a shake can. A calm dog requires a medium-firm tone of voice and no noise corrections from a shake can. All other personality types require a firm "No" and a vigorous rattle of the shake can.

Feeding and Walking Schedule

In a young puppy, the process of housebreaking is helped by setting his biological clock in terms of eating, digesting, and eliminating. Feeding your puppy a precise amount of food at a precise time every day and night helps his biological clock dictate the rhythm of digestion and elimination in a set pattern that helps both dog and owner. Dogs living indoors benefit the most from this approach.

The most interesting part of this method is that you do not take the puppy outside when you think that his food has digested. You take him outside immediately after feeding and watering him. The reason is simple. Every time the puppy eats food or drinks water, it triggers a reflex along the entire digestive tract and sets in motion the complicated mechanics of digestion that end in the elimination of body waste. The scientific term for this is *peristalsis*. By feeding the puppy the same amount of food at the same times each day and by taking him outside to eliminate immediately afterward, you are creating a digestive pattern that will work for the rest of the dog's life.

You will get favorable results with this program by feeding, watering, and walking him at the same times each day. Once you begin to schedule your dog's eating and walking times you actually control when he will relieve himself.

The schedules that follow must be adhered to if the training program is going to be successful. There are several schedules offered as they pertain to the age of your puppy or older dog. Use the one that applies to your situation. These feeding and walking schedules should only be used during the training period. Afterward, they can be adjusted according to your individual needs, the age of your dog, and the advice of your veterinarian as it pertains to your pet's nutritional requirements.

Schedule for Puppies Seven Weeks to Six Months Old

7:00 A.M.	Walk the dog.
7:30 A.M.	Feed, water, and walk.
11:30 A.M.	Feed, water, and walk.
4:30 P.M.	Feed, water, and walk.
8:30 P.M.	Water and walk (last water of the day).
11:30 P.M.	Walk the dog.

Schedule for Puppies Six to Twelve Months Old

7:00 A.M.   Walk the dog.

7:30 A.M.   Feed, water, and walk.

12:30 P.M.   Water and walk.

4:30 P.M.   Feed, water, and walk.

7:30 P.M.   Water and walk (last water of the day).

11:00 P.M.   Walk the dog.

Schedule for Dogs Twelve Months and Older*

7:00 A.M.   Walk the dog.

7:30 A.M.   Feed, water, and walk.

4:30 P.M.   Water and walk.

7:30 P.M.   Water and walk (last water of the day).

11:00 P.M.   Walk the dog.

In some cases a veterinarian will require that a one-year-old or older dog be fed twice a day. In that case add a feeding to the 4:30 P.M. part of the schedule. In that way the animal will have sufficient time to eliminate his final meal before bedding down for the night.

Schedule for Working People (Any Age Dog)*

First thing in the morning	Walk the dog.
Before leaving for work	Feed, water, and walk the dog.
Midday	If possible, have a friend, relative, neighbor, or hired person feed, water, and walk your puppy. (Only water and a walk for a grown dog.)
Home from work	Walk the dog.
Early evening	Water and walk the dog (last water of the day).
Before bedtime	Walk the dog.

When you are at work, keep the dog confined in a designated area, such as the kitchen, with a see-through puppy gate. Do not place newspaper on the floor. Expect accidents. Simply clean them up when you come home and do not correct the dog for them. You may use a wire dog crate providing someone comes in to walk the dog at midday.

Consistency is the most important part of housebreaking. Once you begin the schedule do not vary from it until your puppy is successfully trained. Allow him fifteen minutes to eat his food and then take it away no matter how much he may have left in the bowl. Wait five minutes and then allow him all the water he wants. By waiting five minutes you may prevent a vigorous eater from regurgitating his meal. During the training period, do not allow the puppy to have any food, water, or snack treats between his feeding times. This is important if his body is going to be regulated. However, consult your veterinarian on all matters pertaining to your dog's nutritional needs.

Nighttime Keep the puppy confined for the night. You may have difficulty in the beginning getting your puppy to relieve himself on his scheduled walks. Stay calm. The little dog may not relieve himself for the first few rounds of his feeding/walking schedule. He may even hold out for an entire day. The puppy is being asked to abandon his old way of doing things and do something entirely different for the first time. If the dog has been previously using papers on the floor, take some paper outdoors. Place a sheet of paper that has been soiled with his urine on an acceptable place in the street and let him sniff it. He may quickly get the idea and scent post on the paper. If the dog holds out for more than twenty-four hours, insert a baby-size glycerin suppository in his anus after his feeding and watering. You may also use a paper matchstick. You should definitely get results. After he relieves himself, praise him so that he knows that going outside pleases you.

Getting Rid of the Scent-Posting Odor

When a puppy has an accident in any area of the house—even his own—the spot must be deodorized thoroughly so that he is not drawn back to the scent of his own urine or feces. It is important not to allow scent posts to be established anywhere indoors.

Because it is normal for dogs to scent post their territory with urine and feces, they are continually drawn back to the same places on the floor to relieve themselves. Even when you cannot smell the exact location, he can. His incredible sense of smell combines with his instinct to mark territory, and he keeps soiling in the same places. In order to break this cycle you must obliterate those undetectable odors that remain. They must be neutralized each and every time the animal soils the place, before you forget the exact location.

Most commercial cleaning products will not eliminate the scent of your dog's urine or feces. He can still smell it for many months after you've washed it with detergents, bleaches, and deodorizers of every description. None of these products is strong enough to remove the subtle odor that remains. It can only be accomplished with the use of an odor neutralizer. There are several preparations available in pet-supply stores and pet-supply catalogs. These products do not attempt to cover up the scent with a strong perfume that smells nice. In a chemical reaction odor neutralizers interact with the original odor and destroy it so the dog cannot go back to it. This is very important in housebreaking. Once the dog has had an accident, been corrected, and been shown where to go, he is then thoroughly discouraged from returning to the scene of the crime if the odor has been destroyed.

Each and every time the puppy has an accident in the house it must be cleaned with the odor neutralizer. Follow the instructions on the label of the product. If it is a concentrate, such as Nilodor, place ten drops of it into one quart of hot water. Mop all soiled areas with this mixture. You will notice that the dog does not return to the same location and will have fewer and fewer accidents in the house. Eventually, he will begin to let you know that he needs to go out because that is the only place that has his scent. Be sure to praise him every time he "goes" outdoors. Let him know he has pleased you.

EIGHT

PAPER TRAINING YOUR PUPPY

Paper Training Is Not Housebreaking. Housebreaking Is Not Paper Training.

Paper Training, by Definition

Paper training means your puppy will relieve himself at scheduled intervals, on newspapers that have been spread on the floor in a convenient location in your home. Once the dog has been trained to do this he should not go outdoors to relieve himself. He should always use newspapers, indoors, on the floor.

When you introduce newspapers for toileting purposes you are teaching your puppy to relieve himself on the floor in addition to helping to establish territory and to assert himself through the messages sent by his odor. He will then continually return to the same locations that have his scent on them and relieve himself on top of the original odor. This is called *scent posting* and is an important instinctive behavior for all dogs.

If you choose to paper train your puppy, it means you permit him to relieve himself indoors in addition to expressing his need to claim and reclaim territory in your home by scent posting. A negative result of paper training is that the puppy grows up without the ability or the inclination to control this behavior and develops the habit of scent posting many parts of your home. It is difficult for some dogs to confine their eliminating behavior to one area of the house after they have been paper trained. After all, they have been taught to relieve themselves on the floor.

The worst situation for a puppy is to have been given newspapers to use on the floor for a week or two and then have them suddenly taken away. The dog then gets hollered at and punished for continuing to use the floor simply because his family now wants him to go outdoors. This merely confuses him. We suggest you choose to either paper train or housebreak your dog, but not both. Also, we believe paper training is only a practical option for toy breeds and small dogs, which do not need as much outdoor exercise as larger breeds.

How to Paper Train Your Dog

This method is most effective for puppies and dogs between the ages of seven weeks and three years, yet is often effective for dogs as old as twelve years. The techniques for paper training are based on six easy elements: (1) Proper diet, (2) Confinement to one area, (3) Newspapers on the floor, (4) Correction, (5) Feeding and papering schedule, and (6) Getting rid of the scent-posting odor. When paper training your dog, walking him is not part of the process. You may walk your dog for pleasure and exercise whenever it is convenient. The period of training could last between two days and two weeks, depending on your dog.

Proper Diet

Select the right dog food. It is best to select a premium dog food formulated for your puppy's age range that says on the label "complete and balanced," or words to that effect. Do not feed your dog leftovers; this does not work with the feeding schedule we suggest. If your puppy develops digestion problems, such as diarrhea, during the training process, it will not work. It is important that you feed your dog properly if the paper-training process is going to be successful.

Confinement to One Area

Do not give your puppy the run of the house until you are satisfied that he is completely paper trained. During this training period, the puppy must always be watched so that he can be corrected in the middle of an accident. Most puppies will try to avoid soiling an area where they must eat and sleep. Establish an area where you can confine the puppy. The most convenient location is the kitchen, which should be large enough that your dog does not feel he is being punished when placed there. Install a see-through puppy gate. Do not use a folding gate for a small puppy, because he is small enough to scoot out at the bottom. Never tie your dog down with a rope, chain, or leash when you leave the house. The area of confinement may also be a wire dog crate conveniently placed where the dog can see what's going on around him. He should not remain in the crate for longer than two or three hours at a time, however. Every time you return home, allow your puppy to leave the confined area; clean up any soiled papers (saving one sheet with which to attract him to a specific place on the floor, as explained on page 137); and praise the dog for having used the papers. Do not allow him to run loose in the house if you cannot watch him 100 percent of the time, because that is when the accidents will occur. If he has accidents that you have not witnessed, you cannot correct him, and you must not punish him at all. Only correct him if you catch him in the act.

Newspapers on the Floor

Spread a three- to five-sheet layer of newspaper over the *entire* kitchen floor. This is where the dog is to be taken when it is time for him to relieve himself. Every time the puppy relieves himself on the papers remove them, but save one sheet that he has marked with his odor. This sheet should be placed underneath the fresh paper on a location that you eventually want him to confine this activity to, such as a corner of the room or close to the sink. The scent will draw him back to that spot when he's ready to go again. Keep the floor covered with paper at all times. Change the papers every time they become soiled. Do this for five days. Begin reducing the area covered by the newspapers by 20 percent every other day. Do this until only an area of floor large enough for the dog to relieve himself on is covered. The entire process should not take more than ten days.

Correction

You must never punish your dog, especially by hitting him or rubbing his nose in his own mess simply because he has made a mistake. You must correct the dog only when you catch him in the middle of his mistake. Puppies should be paper trained with a firm verbal correction and a noise correction immediately followed by lavish praise. Praising your dog for doing the right thing is the key to success. See Chapter Seven, Housebreaking Your Puppy, "How to Correct Your Dog."

Feeding and Papering Schedule

By placing your puppy's feeding time on a specific schedule, you can control when he will relieve himself. It usually takes food from six to eight hours to pass through his system. You will get favorable results with this program by feeding, watering, and papering him at the same times each day. If the puppy is fed in the same area or room with his papers, you will only have to take the food and water away when it's time for him to relieve himself. If he is fed in a different room, he must be taken to his papered area when it is time.

You must adhere to the following schedule if the training program is going to be successful.

Schedule for Puppies Seven Weeks to Six Months Old

7:00 A.M.	Paper the dog.
7:30 A.M.	Feed, water, and paper.
11:30 A.M.	Feed, water, and paper.
4:30 P.M.	Feed, water, and paper.
8:30 P.M.	Water and paper (last water of the day).
11:30 P.M.	Paper the dog.

Schedule for Puppies Six to Twelve Months Old

7:00 A.M.	Paper the dog.
7:30 A.M.	Feed, water, and paper.
12:30 P.M.	Water and paper.
4:30 P.M.	Feed, water, and paper.
7:30 P.M.	Water and paper (last water of the day).
11:00 P.M.	Paper the dog.

Schedule for Dogs Twelve Months and Older*

7:00 A.M.	Paper the dog.
7:30 A.M.	Feed, water, and paper.
4:30 P.M.	Water and paper.
7:30 P.M.	Water and paper (last water of the day).
11:00 P.M.	Paper the dog.

*In some cases a veterinarian will require that a one-year-old or older dog be fed twice a day. In that case add a feeding to the 4:30 P.M. part of the schedule. That way the animal will have sufficient time to eliminate his final meal before bedding down for the night.

Schedule for Working People (Any Age Dog)

First thing in the morning	Paper the dog.
Soon after first papering	Feed, water, and paper.
Before leaving for work	Place clean papers on the floor; keep the dog confined.
Home from work	Clean up soiled papers.* Feed, water, and paper.
Before bedtime	Paper the dog (no food or water).

Do not correct the dog for soiled papers when you arrive home from work.

Getting Rid of the Scent-Posting Odor

Because it is normal for dogs to scent post their territory with urine and feces, they are continually drawn back to the same places on the floor to relieve themselves. More often than not they will eliminate on the same spot again and again. Even when you cannot smell the exact location, your dog can. In order to break this cycle you must obliterate those undetectable odors that remain in places other than your dog's papering area. They must be neutralized each and every time he soils in the wrong place. Most commercial cleaning products will not eliminate the scent of your dog's urine or feces. He can still smell it for many months after you've washed it with numerous detergents, bleaches, and deodorizers. None of these products is strong enough to remove the subtle odor that remains.

To fully get rid of the scent, you will need to use an odor neutralizer. These products do not attempt to cover up the scent with a strong, sweet-smelling perfume, and you can find them in many pet-supply stores, catalogs, or on the Internet. In a chemical reaction, odor neutralizers interact with the original odor and destroy it so the dog will not be drawn back to it. This is very important in paper training. Once the dog has had an accident, been corrected, and been shown where to go, he is thoroughly discouraged from returning to the scene of the crime if the odor has been eliminated. Each and every time the puppy soils an area of the house that is not his papering area, it must be cleaned with the odor neutralizer. Follow the instructions on the label of the product. Praise him every time he uses the papering area. Let him know he has pleased you.

NINE

TRAINING YOUR PUPPY

Dog training, or obedience training, is a method of communicating with your puppy and teaching him to understand and accept human dominance. If a puppy is to live a happy and successful life as a pet, he must behave in a manner that is acceptable to humans. Dog training is based on the canine instinct to live in a social framework called the *pack*. A pack is a family or team of dogs (or wolves) that lives and works together for its survival. Pet dogs transfer this instinct to humans and think of family life as a substitute pack. The pack always has leaders and followers. It is essential that humans be the leaders and pets be the followers. Dog training establishes this.

If done properly, dog training will make a puppy happier because of the emotional security it provides. It brings order out of chaos and appeals to the dog's instinct for pack survival. The canine mentality thrives on family life, leaders and followers, and a safe place to live.

Professional trainers base their methods on the dog's acceptance of the human's position of dominance and the animal's desire to please. After a dog is taught an obedience command, he is rewarded when the command is performed properly and corrected when it is not.

Dog training is based on specific teaching techniques and the reinforcement of those techniques. Reinforcements are like reminders and involve rewards and corrections. In our method, a reward is verbal praise from the dog's owner or trainer. It is given every time the dog executes a command properly. It is also given after every *correction*.

A correction is a message that communicates to the puppy that he did the wrong thing or failed to obey a command. There are *verbal corrections, noise corrections,* and *leash corrections*. A verbal correction is simply the word *No* said in a firm tone of voice. A noise correction is a harsh sound made by rattling a shake can (see Chapter Four). A leash correction is a quick pull on a leather leash attached to a training collar.

About This Training Method

In this chapter you will be shown how to teach your puppy the fundamental commands of dog training. The commands are SIT, SIT-STAY, HEEL and AUTOMATIC SIT, DOWN, DOWN-STAY, and COME. If you learn when and how to effectively praise or correct your puppy, in addition to these commands, you will have at your fingertips the basic means of communicating with him. The use of praise and correction is the language of dogs and people.

A professional trainer or a knowledgeable pet owner must know the basics of dog behavior to successfully train a puppy. Please refer to Chapter Five to understand more about dog behavior. The objective of dog training is to control your puppy's behavior in such a way that the bond between you is strengthened and actually turns into a loving relationship. The key elements are patience and understanding. *A puppy should not be trained with the same firmness as a mature dog and requires more time to learn.* Training can begin as early as seven weeks of age, but must be tailored to the dog's age, temperament, size, and rate of learning.

Do not forget that your main concern is to create a bond between your puppy and the family. You must control your temper even when you become frustrated, and you will. Learn to control your voice so that you are gently demanding and not harsh, suggestive and not pushy, cheerful and not hysterical or dictatorial. Keep in mind that you must first teach a puppy what you want before you can expect him to do it, and *never* punish him for not obeying your commands. There is the possibility that something may be lacking in your teaching efforts if the training does not work.

Please note that the photos and their captions in this chapter explain the training techniques in the most specific way. The text within the chapter provides useful information about each command in a more general way. Pay careful attention to the photos and their captions when training your puppy. It is true that one picture is worth a thousand words.

Getting Started
•
The Training Collar and the Leather Leash

The right way to place the training collar around your puppy's neck.

The wrong way to place the training collar around your puppy's neck.

The training collar is a short length of highly polished chain, with small metal links and a large ring at each end. It is an important tool for communicating with your puppy. By properly looping the chain through one of the large rings, you form a slip knot that is wide enough to slide over the puppy's head.

Here's how to do it: Hold one end of the slip collar by the ring with your left hand. The collar will fall into a vertical line. Grab the bottom ring with your right hand. Work the chain through the bottom ring so that it begins to form a slip knot. Allow the chain to drop through the bottom ring. This will create a loop that goes around the puppy's neck.

To place the loop over the puppy's neck properly, the ring in your left hand should point away from his right side. *The collar must tighten around the puppy's neck when pulled and loosen when released.* It is essential that the collar slide back and forth smoothly and quickly for the sake of his comfort.

When placing the slip collar over the head, you are doing it correctly if it looks like the letter *P* around the puppy's neck. When incorrect, the slip collar resembles the number 9 on the left and the number 6 on the right; it will not slide back and forth as it should. If the puppy is facing you, place the collar on him so the ring that will attach to the leash is on the left side of his neck.

Attach the leash clip to the outstanding large ring. Both puppy and trainer are now ready for a lesson. Like any slip knot, the chain will tighten around the puppy's neck when the leash is pulled gently. When this is done the puppy experiences a mild, negative sensation. If the word *No* always accompanies this mild sensation, he will learn this means that he has not performed properly. Release the tension immediately after pulling the leash so the collar does not stay tightened around the puppy's neck.

Holding the Leash Properly
for the Leash Correction

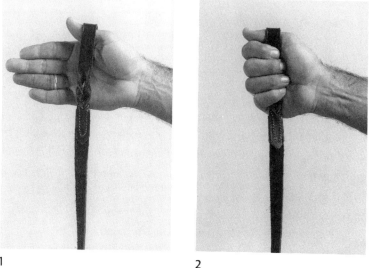

1   2

Holding the leash properly.

With the training collar around your puppy's neck, and a six-
foot leash attached to it, place the thumb of your right hand
through the top loop of the leash. Stand to the puppy's right, the
two of you facing the same direction. With your left hand, bring
the middle of the leash over to the right, wrapping it around
the right thumb over the loop. Half the leash is in your right
hand, while half hangs loosely between your right hand and the
puppy's collar. Close the fingers of your right hand and clench
the leash firmly with your palm facing up. Placing your left hand
under your right, clench the gathered leash with your left palm
facing down for reinforcement of the grip.

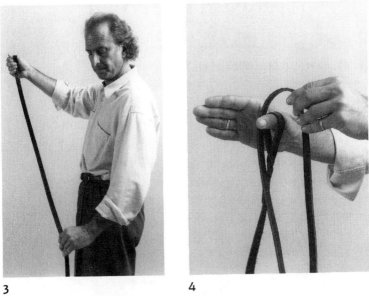

3

4

5

How to Administer a Leash Correction

It is important to understand that not every puppy is the same. They vary in temperament and therefore require a different approach to leash corrections, depending on their age, size, sensitivity, and temperament. Please refer to Chapter Three to determine how to adjust leash corrections to the needs of your puppy.

Once the puppy has demonstrated that he has learned what you have taught him, it is fair to correct him if he does not obey, or does the wrong thing. In dog training, he must respond on

Leash Correction 1. Hold the leash with both hands a bit below waist level.

Leash Correction 2. Jerk the leash sideways and slightly upward to the right. When the leash is jerked, the training collar tightens around the puppy's neck, giving him a mild, negative sensation. As you jerk the leash say "No" in a firm tone of voice.

Leash Correction 3. Return to the original position. Do not jerk a puppy too hard. When your hands return, the collar automatically loosens. Once the puppy has responded to the leash correction and has obeyed your command or stopped an offensive action, you must praise him generously. Let your puppy know that he has pleased you. One must encourage a dog by praising him every step of the way. That is positive reinforcement of the teaching process.

command. If your dog does not respond properly, you should give him a mild correction using the leash correction. That is negative reinforcement.

Correct your puppy by jerking the leash when he refuses to obey or does the wrong thing. Say "No" in a firm tone of voice. Release the tension on the leash instantly and then praise him affectionately. For a more detailed explanation, see accompanying photos.

Communicating with Your Puppy

The correct use of your voice is crucial to the successful control of your puppy's behavior. Dogs do not understand English; it is the tone of your voice to which they respond. The sounds you make and the words you use are essential tools for training.

The goal is to modify your puppy's behavior. It is accomplished by correcting him firmly and by praising him lavishly as he stops doing the wrong thing. Of course, the puppy should be praised if he does the correct thing in the first place.

The word *No,* when delivered in a commanding, authoritative tone of voice, tells the puppy you mean business and is a vital method for teaching him how to behave. You must be able to convince him that you are in control. Most dogs respond instantly to commands spoken clearly in a firm tone of voice.

You must be able to exaggerate the sound of your voice in order to teach your puppy right from wrong. Modify your vocal pitch and tone so that there is a great difference between an enthusiastic and loving "Good dog" and an authoritative "Down."

Two words are used as vocal tools to communicate with your puppy: *No* and *Obey. No* is used to stop him when he misbehaves or does not perform correctly. Use it consistently to indicate your disapproval; don't confuse him with other words, such as *Don't* or *Stop.* Pronounce the word positively and clearly so that it implies your authority and strength. It is equally important not to associate your dog's name with the negativism of *No.* For this reason, never say "Philly, no." Do not repeat the word to get a response. Your dog should respond to one *No.* When you repeat the word over and over, you only reduce its impact.

The word *Okay* is a positive command of anticipation or release. Use it as a positive prefix to your dog's name ("Okay, Philly, Come!") You should also use it as a release from training sessions or a release from walking at your side outdoors to relieve himself. Saying "Okay" is like saying class is dismissed. *Okay* is associated with freedom and release and should never be used negatively.

Leash Breaking Your Puppy

You cannot obedience train a puppy without a leash. Some puppies accept the leash immediately, while others resist it because they are frightened or not used to it. Do not wait to put a leash on your new dog. To get your puppy to accept a leash without much fuss, use a buckled collar and attach a *lightweight* leash to it. You can even use a heavy string or four-foot clothesline if you like. Allow the dog to drag the leash around all day so that he'll become used to it. *Important: To avoid accidents, never leave the puppy alone with the leash attached to him.*

After seven days of dragging the leash around, he should have become adjusted to it. Be certain the buckled collar is comfortable. Always be cheerful and upbeat when attaching the leash to the collar.

Pick up the leash many times a day during the seven-day leash-breaking period. Be relaxed as you do it, and apply no tension to the line, as you would if you were taking him out for a walk.

Leash Breaking 1. Many puppies refuse to walk when the leash is attached for the first time.

Leash Breaking 2. Leash resistance may be expressed three ways: by the paws, the mouth, or the teeth. If a puppy paws the leash or bites it, say "No" firmly and pull the leash away. Do not forget to praise your dog after the voice correction.

Leash Breaking 3. If your puppy refuses to walk while on-leash, kneel and call him to you in a happy, loving tone of voice.

Leash Breaking 4. When the little dog finally comes to you, praise him lavishly. Try to create a pleasant association with the leash.

If the puppy rejects the leash by pawing it or biting it, say "No" in a firm tone of voice and pull it out of his mouth. After each voice correction, praise the puppy generously.

Once your puppy seems to have made an adjustment to the leash in the house, try walking outdoors. It is best to begin on a soft, grassy surface. If he resists walking on-leash, the grass will prevent his paws from painfully scraping against the sidewalk.

Teaching the Command *Sit*

SIT and SIT-STAY are two different commands and must be taught at separate times. The goal of SIT is to teach your dog to sit on your command, and it is the easiest command to teach. To accomplish this you will need a training collar and a six-foot leather leash.

Start out by attaching the leash to the collar and placing your thumb through the leash loop. This prevents the puppy from

SIT 1. Kneel next to your puppy, by his right side.

SIT 2. Grasp the hip joints or hip sockets of your puppy, which are at the base of his spine. When you feel two indentations, press them firmly, but gently, with your fingers.

yanking the leash out of your hand. Keep the leash short by gathering it up in your right hand, allowing approximately two feet of it to remain between the collar and your hand. This gives you maximum control without pulling the puppy.

The photos explain each step of administering the SIT command. At some point, as you repeat the technique shown in the photos, your dog will begin to sit at your command without any hand or leash pressure. The length of time this will take varies with the age, temperament, and breed of your puppy.

Once the puppy seems to understand what is expected of him, try giving the command without using your hand to push him into the proper position. Say "Sit" and gently raise the leash with your right hand. Praise him each and every time he goes into the SIT position.

SIT 3. Tell your puppy to SIT, stretching the word out, as in "S-I-I-I-T." While you say SIT, use your hands to guide him into a sitting position by pushing down with your left hand on his hips and pulling the leash up with your right hand at the same time.

SIT 4. Stretching the word out, as explained, adjust the pitch of your voice to sound cheerful, gentle, and reassuring. Once your dog is in the SIT position, praise him enthusiastically, even though your hands helped him. Repeat this procedure until the puppy begins to sit on your command, without the use of your hands.

Next, eliminate the pull-up with the leash. Say "Sit" and do not apply any hand or leash pressure. Praise the puppy lavishly each time he obeys the command properly.

Once you feel your puppy understands the command you may use a leash correction if he fails to obey or perform properly. Repeat each step of the teaching techniques approximately ten or fifteen times. If your puppy seems to be getting tired, end the session and allow him to have some water, relieve himself, and take a nap. You may give him two training sessions a day, but space them four hours apart.

Teaching the Command *Sit·Stay*

The goal of this command is to teach your puppy to STAY while he is in the SIT position until you release him from the command. To teach this command you will need a training collar and a six-foot leather leash. The command involves three techniques: a verbal command, a hand signal that blocks the dog's vision, and a pivotal turn on the ball of your left foot.

Refer to the photos for step-by-step instructions on administering the SIT-STAY command. Once your puppy has learned to remain in SIT-STAY at a distance of six feet from you, you can reinforce his ability to obey the command in different ways.

Walking Around Both Sides of the Puppy as He Remains in STAY

The goal is to teach the young dog to remain in SIT-STAY, without moving, as you walk to either side of him.

Place the puppy in SIT. Give him the command STAY. Use the hand signal and execute the pivotal turn as you hold the leash tautly above his head. Once you are standing in front of the dog, take one or two steps to the right as you hold the dog in place. Return to the original position directly in front of him. Now do the same to the left. Return to original position. Repeat this twelve times. Having accomplished this, repeat the entire lesson up to this point five or ten times, until you are satisfied that the puppy has absorbed everything.

Walking Around the Puppy as He Remains in SIT-STAY

The goal is to extend the puppy's ability to obey the SIT-STAY command while you are out of his direct line of sight.

Review all elements of SIT-STAY. Then, turn toward the puppy and back away from him to the end of the leash. During the procedure, remind him to STAY and then praise him for obeying.

SIT-STAY 1. *The verbal command.* With the puppy on your left side, both you and the animal are facing in the same direction. Give him the command SIT. Praise him after he goes into the proper position.

SIT-STAY 2. *The hand signal.* Give your puppy the command STAY! The hand signal accompanies the verbal command. Hold the leash with your right hand and allow enough to drape across your knees so there is a little slack. Give the hand signal by flattening your left hand and keeping all fingers straight and close together, as if you were going to go swimming. As you give the command STAY, place your left hand in front of the puppy's eyes, leaving about four inches of space, careful never to touch his eyes. The hand signal is done quickly and blocks his vision for a second only. Return your left hand to your side one or two seconds after blocking his vision. Eventually, the puppy should remain in the STAY position with the use of the hand signal only.

SIT-STAY 3. *The pivotal turn on the left foot.* The goal is to make a pivotal turn so that you will face the dog without causing him to stir. To accomplish this, use your left foot as a pivot and do not move it from its original position.

Step off with your right foot and turn to face the puppy. Allow your left foot to pivot in place as your right foot moves forward one step so that you are almost facing the dog. At the same time that you turn around, keep the leash above your puppy's head, careful to hold it to one side so that you do not hit him on the chin. Keep the leash tight enough to restrain the dog's movements. If you do this in any other way, the dog will assume you are about to move forward and start to go with you.

SIT-STAY 4. After you have placed the right foot on the ground, toes facing the puppy, move the left foot next to it so that you have made a complete turn and are now facing him. You may lower the leash slightly, but keep it taut. Stand in front of the puppy for about thirty seconds while he remains in the STAY position. Praise him generously for his cor-rect response. The pivotal turn is merely a teaching tool and will not be used after the dog has learned the command completely.

SIT-STAY 5. Back away three feet from the puppy. The goal is to teach him to remain in SIT-STAY at a distance of three feet until he is released from the command. While holding the leash above his head, shift it to the left hand, placing the thumb inside the loop at the top. The right hand then grasps the main line of the leash about halfway down and holds it loosely, directly under the left hand. As you back away, the leash should be able to slide freely through the right hand allowing it to extend, which will prevent any slack from developing as you back away.

Start backing away from the puppy. Let the leash slide through your right hand as you hold it firmly with your left so it gets longer as you move backward. He may begin to walk toward you as you move away; if he does, give him the verbal command STAY and move toward him. Pull the leash through your right hand as you move forward and hold it once again above his head. Stepping toward him will stop him from moving. Praise him once he has stopped moving. Pause for several seconds and then begin backing away again until you are three feet away. Praise him once you reach the desired three feet and hold the position for thirty seconds. Repeat the process fifteen times.

SIT-STAY 6. Back away six feet from the puppy and repeat the procedure shown in the previous photo. Continue walking backward slowly, one step at a time. After each step, remind the puppy to STAY and praise him for doing so. At some point during this gradual backing away from him, the puppy will probably jump toward you. When he does, you should command him to STAY and simultaneously step forward to block him, shortening the leash through your right hand, holding it tautly above his head for control. As soon as he sits down, praise him generously, pause for several seconds, and then begin backing away again until you reach the full limit of the leash. At that distance, remain standing in front of him for thirty seconds. Practice this command at least twelve times.

Keeping the leash high and taut, move a foot to the right; stop and praise the dog. Reverse directions and move to the left, increasing the distance to two feet. Praise the dog for staying in position with a soft, soothing tone.

Continue moving from right to left, gradually increasing your distance in each direction. The puppy is permitted to turn his head to follow your movements, but not his body. If he tries to turn, you must stop him. Step forward, tighten the leash, and tell him to STAY.

When you have reached the full limit of the leash, stand at a 180-degree angle, in front of the dog, then walk back and forth from side to side twelve times. Let your puppy know how much his performance pleases you.

Next, slowly start walking around him. At frequent intervals, call out to him to STAY. When you have completed a full circle, stop and praise him.

The key to your control during your circling of the dog is firm leash control. When the puppy tries to move, quickly pull up on the leash, reminding him to STAY.

Teaching the Commands *Heel* and *Automatic Sit*
•
Heel

Limit each session to fifteen minutes and conduct no more than two sessions a day, spaced at least four hours apart. Practice walking in HEEL every time you take your puppy out to relieve himself.

A dog should be at least three months old before he is taught to HEEL. While it is possible to teach the command to a frisky young puppy, you risk damaging his emerging personality, since the command goes against his natural curiosity and instinct to run free.

For step-by-step instructions on teaching the command HEEL, see accompanying photos. The correct position for HEEL is with your puppy on your left side, just about next to your left knee. After several lessons it becomes important that he maintain the proper position. In the early lessons the puppy will have done all right if he stayed only two or three feet ahead. However, by the third lesson he must be corrected whenever he strays from your side.

HEEL 1. Attach the puppy's collar and leash. Standing to his right, gather approximately one third of the leash in your right hand, while the remainder of the leash hangs between your hand and his collar. Both arms should be relaxed.

HEEL 2. Say your puppy's name, followed by the word Heel, emphasizing the command word. HEEL is an action command, requiring forward motion. Your puppy's name is a signal alerting him to watch you and prepare to move. As you say the command word HEEL, step forward on your left foot, which is closest to the dog and will get him moving the instant you do.

HEEL 3. Allow your puppy to run ahead of you.

HEEL 4. As the puppy gets to the end of the fully extended leash, grasp it with both hands and administer a leash correction. Stop walking forward. Make a fast U-turn, and as you do, say the command HEEL, in a firm tone of voice. Walk briskly in the opposite direction. The dog will be startled and forcibly turned in the direction you are walking.

HEEL 5. As he approaches you, pat your thigh to encourage him to come close and praise him when he reaches your side. After a correction, your puppy may approach and then run past you. Should this occur, begin this exercise again.

Whenever the puppy fails to maintain the exact position, do the following: Administer a leash correction by gently jerking the leash to the side. Use the dog's name; say, "Philly, HEEL," execute a U-turn, and walk in the opposite direction. Give the puppy immediate praise. The praise lets the dog know that you are not angry and that he is now doing the correct thing. *Remember to gauge the strength of the leash correction to the size, temperament, and age of your dog. Do not overdo it for a young, fragile dog.*

Walking in HEEL is not a natural instinct for any dog, much less a puppy. In addition to his confusion, a puppy may also be frightened when going out for the first time. You must realize this and be especially patient and understanding. Be gentle and easygoing, and keep your tone of voice cheerful and energetic to encourage him to perform correctly.

Your puppy may be startled when you first correct him for failing to walk in HEEL. He will most probably pull ahead or lag behind. Although you must be firm, you must also be considerate because he is, after all, only a puppy. Select an enclosed area that is distraction-free, with sufficient room to walk back and forth.

Some puppies tend to lag behind and will make their first HEEL lessons a series of stops and starts. This may be a result of the leash correction given for running ahead. Talking to your puppy is the best answer to this problem. Playfully encourage the little dog to walk with you, to catch up, to keep pace. If the sound of your voice is enthusiastic and friendly, the puppy will bound to you and this is exactly what you want.

If necessary, kneel and call the dog to you. When he reaches you, rise quickly and begin walking in the original direction. If the puppy does not respond properly, you may gently snap the leash with a slight jerk or pull. What you want is for your puppy to pay attention to *you* when he is taken for a walk.

The Automatic Sit

The AUTOMATIC SIT means your puppy will respond to a stop when walking in HEEL by going directly into a SIT position. The dog will stop every time you do and SIT without being commanded to do so.

You accomplish this by alerting the dog that a stop is coming up. The signal for stopping is simply a reduction of your walking

AUTOMATIC SIT 1. Tell your puppy to HEEL and begin to walk at a moderate speed. After a couple of minutes, gradually slow down, and he will slow down, too. Stop completely and tell the puppy to SIT.

AUTOMATIC SIT 3. Tell your puppy, "S-I-I-I-T," stretching the word out on the vowel sound. While you say the command, use your hands to guide him into a sitting position. As you push down with your left hand on his hips, pull the leash up with your right hand.

AUTOMATIC SIT 2. Depending on your puppy's size, kneel or bend over next to him, on his right side. Grasp his hip joints or hip sockets at the base of his spine. You will feel two indentations. Press them firmly but gently with your fingers.

AUTOMATIC SIT 4. Once the puppy is in the SIT position, praise him lavishly even though you placed him there. Repeat this procedure until the puppy begins to sit automatically, without a verbal command.

speed. If the dog is focused on you, he will be sensitive to any change of pace. As you slow down, so will the puppy.

For step-by-step instructions on teaching the AUTOMATIC SIT command, see photos. During the teaching process, give the puppy the command SIT every time you stop. As you verbally give the command, raise the leash tautly above his head. Assuming he has already learned the command SIT, that is all that should be necessary. This may not be the case with an exuberant puppy, however. Repeat this procedure many times until he sits without the verbal command. Never use the dog's name when giving this command, because SIT is not an action command. Every time the dog sits on command, give him his well-deserved praise.

If the puppy does not SIT after he has been taught to do so, you may administer a leash correction and a firm "No" immediately followed by praise. If the puppy does not respond properly to leash corrections, repeat the teaching techniques for SIT until he performs properly.

Teaching the Commands
Down and *Down-Stay*
·
Down

DOWN means a puppy will lower his entire body to the ground or floor, on command. All dogs and puppies prefer to lie down when they are tired or bored. However, lying down on command is not a natural behavior and greatly inhibits a puppy's freedom. As a result, many dogs and puppies resist learning this command. Some aggressive dogs may even growl or snap during the teaching process. It is a difficult command to teach and requires extra repetition, time, patience, and effort. Still, the rewards are well worth the added effort. A puppy that will respond properly to DOWN and DOWN-STAY can be much easier to control than one that won't.

For step-by-step instructions for teaching the DOWN command, see photos. Because this training course is designed for puppies it is best to use one basic teaching method for DOWN, the *Hand*

DOWN 1. The Hand Technique. Place your puppy in SIT-STAY on your left side, and face the same direction as the dog. With both hands, hold the leash. It should extend upward from his collar, across your left thigh, to your hands, which should be in the center of your body, near your waistline. By not allowing any slack in the leash, you will prevent him from moving around or playing. If he tries to move away, tighten the leash, give him the command SIT, and then praise him.

Technique. However, a variation of that technique is also included as an alternative. The variation is the *Paws Technique,* which is useful for puppies that resist the Hand Technique. Most puppies can be taught with either of the two techniques but it is best to start out using the Hand Technique. If your dog resists, then switch to the Paws Technique, but never use the Paws Technique for high-energy or aggressive puppies. *After teaching one or the other of these techniques you must continue on to the* Front Technique *and the* Front Technique from a Greater Distance. *This is essential.*

DOWN 2. *The Hand Technique.* Stand next to your puppy; kneel next to him if he is small. Flatten your left hand and close all your fingers together. Raise your left hand slightly above the eye level of the puppy and to the right of his head, and make sure there is no slack in the leash.

DOWN 3. *The Hand Technique.* Say the command DOWN, and lower your left hand toward the ground. In doing so, the flat of your palm will hit the top of the leash about where the clip connects to the collar. The verbal command should be stretched on the vowel sound as you lower your hand as well as the pitch of your voice: "D-O-O-W-W-N."

Down-Stay

DOWN-STAY means your puppy remains in the DOWN position on the ground or floor until you release him from the command. DOWN-STAY is similar to SIT-STAY, and the teaching technique is almost the same with only a few differences. *For complete instructions, see photos.* Do not use the puppy's name when giving the verbal command STAY. If the dog has already been taught SIT-STAY, then you can safely assume that he knows

DOWN 4. *The Hand Technique.* When your palm reaches the puppy's neck, press down on the leash at the collar. Unless your puppy is very large, the downward pressure from your palm will push him down, into the proper position.

DOWN 5. *The Hand Technique.* Your puppy, through his peripheral vision, can see your left hand push him into the DOWN position, which he will associate with lowering his body to the ground. This is also how he learns to respond to your proper hand signal. Repeat this procedure at least fifteen times, or as many times as necessary to lower the dog without any resistance.

DOWN 1. *The Paws Technique.*
Kneel to your puppy's right
side and face the same direction. Command him to SIT-
STAY and praise him for
obeying.

DOWN 2. *The Paws Technique.*
While kneeling on your left
knee, say the command
DOWN, drawing it out softly
on the vowel and dropping
your pitch as you pronounce
it: "D-O-O-W-W-N." Gently hold
the puppy's two front paws
with your free hand, and place
your middle finger between the
two paws so that they do not
get pressed painfully together.

DOWN 3. *The Paws Technique.*
As you give the verbal command, gently lift the puppy's front paws off the ground and place them in front of him. This takes away his support, which gently forces him to fall into the DOWN position. Repeat this action fifteen times or until he goes down with almost no resistance at all.

DOWN 1. *The Front Technique.*
After completing either the Hand Technique or the Paws Technique you must continue with these next two techniques for teaching DOWN.

DOWN 2. *The Front Technique.*
This is an important step in reinforcing your puppy's knowledge of the hand signal. Push the top of the leash downward as your arm lowers.

Now that the puppy has learned to be pushed into DOWN by your hand from the side, it is safe to assume that you can do it from the front. With the dog in SIT-STAY, turn about-face and stand in front of him. Hold the leash taut and slightly above his head with one hand, and raise the other hand with the fingers extended straight and close to each other.

DOWN 3. *The Front Technique.* The lowering of your hand on the leash must be accompanied with the verbal command DOWN. As your voice stretches and lowers in tone, the dog is actually pushed to the ground.

DOWN 4. *The Front Technique.* At this point your puppy will probably drop DOWN by himself. If he does, praise him enthusiastically and then repeat the exercise fifteen times. In any case, praise the dog the instant he is all the way down.

DOWN-STAY. STAY in the DOWN position may confuse some dogs, and they will need more lessons. In that case, go back to the SIT-STAY section on page 156 and repeat those lessons.

DOWN 1. *The Front Technique from a Greater Distance.* Place your puppy in SIT-STAY and get in front of him, standing as far back from him as he can tolerate without moving; with some puppies the distance will be two feet, three feet, or perhaps six feet. Hold the leash with your left hand and tighten it slightly above his head if he tries to move away. Raise your right hand straight up with the fingers close together. Give the verbal command DOWN, stretching out the word and using the descending tone of voice.

DOWN 2. *The Front Technique from a Greater Distance.* Lower your right arm as you say the command. Allow the flattened right hand, palm down, to land on top of the leash.

DOWN 3. *The Front Technique from a Greater Distance.* Continue pressing down until the leash touches the floor.

DOWN 4. *The Front Technique from a Greater Distance.* Praise the puppy for going DOWN into the proper position. Repeat this procedure fifteen times, or until he drops to the floor without resistance.

An important next step is to repeat the entire Front Technique from a Greater Distance but *do not* touch the leash with your hand as your arm is lowered. Allow your hand to brush past the leash without actually touching it. This will be exactly the way your hand signal will look from a distance, once the puppy has learned to respond perfectly to the command. Repeat this phase until he obeys the command DOWN perfectly from both your verbal command and hand signal.

DOWN-STAY 1. *The verbal command.* With the puppy on your left side, both you and your puppy face the same direction. Give him the command SIT; praise him. Give him the command DOWN; praise him.

DOWN-STAY 2. *The hand signal.* Give your puppy the command STAY! The hand signal accompanies the verbal command. Hold the leash with your right hand and allow enough to drape across your knees so there is a little slack.

Give the signal with your left hand, flattening it and keeping all fingers straight and close together. As you give the command STAY, place your left hand about four inches in front of the puppy's eyes, careful never to touch them. The hand signal is accomplished quickly and blocks his vision for an instant. Return your left hand to your side one or two seconds after blocking the dog's vision. Eventually, he will remain in the STAY position with the use of the hand signal exclusively.

DOWN-STAY 3. *The pivotal turn on the left foot.* The goal is to make a pivotal turn so that you will face the puppy without causing him to stir. Maintain the hand signal throughout the following motion; use the left foot as a pivot and do not move it from its original position. Step off with your right foot and turn to face the puppy.

Allow your left foot to pivot in place as your right foot moves forward one step so that you are almost facing the dog. At the same time that you turn around, keep the leash above his head, tight enough to restrain the dog's movements. If you do this in any other way, he will assume you are about to move forward and will start to go with you.

DOWN-STAY 4. After you have placed your right foot on the ground, toes facing the puppy, move the left foot next to it so that you have accomplished the complete turn and are now facing him straight on. Stand in front of the puppy for about thirty seconds while he remains in the STAY position, and praise him generously for his correct response. The pivotal turn is merely a teaching tool and will not be used after he has learned the command completely.

DOWN-STAY 5. Slowly back away until you are approximately six feet from the puppy. The goal is to teach him to remain in DOWN-STAY from a distance of six feet until he is released from the command. While holding the leash, shift it to your left hand, placing the thumb inside the loop at the top. With your right hand, grasp the main line of the leash about halfway down and hold it loosely, directly under the left hand. As you back away, the leash should be able to slide freely through the right hand, to extend to full length. This prevents any slack from developing as you back away.

Start backing away. The leash slides through your right hand as you hold it firmly with your left, and gets longer as you move backward. The puppy may begin to walk toward you as you move away. If he does, give him the verbal command STAY and move toward him. Pull the leash through your right hand as you move forward and hold it once again above his head.

Stepping toward him will stop him from moving, and once he stops moving, he must be praised. Pause for several seconds and then begin backing away again until you are six feet away. Praise him once you reach the desired distance and hold the position for thirty seconds. Repeat the process fifteen times.

Teaching the Command *Come*

COME means your puppy must respond instantly when you call him. Responding to the command, he stops what he is doing, runs to the one who has called him, and places himself in a SIT position when he reaches his destination.

For step-by-step instructions for teaching the command COME, see accompanying photos. COME should be taught indoors, and outdoors, providing conditions are safe, controlled, and free of any hazard. This command should not be used off-leash outdoors. Letting a dog loose outdoors is very risky, and some of the best-disciplined dogs have on occasion failed to respond to COME and have gotten into accidents. Still, the command is useful indoors and is well worth the teaching effort.

COME WHEN CALLED 1. Place your puppy in a SIT-STAY position. Back away from him slowly until you reach the full extent of the leash. Face the puppy from a six-foot distance and give him the verbal command, "Okay, Prince, Come." Draw out the "O-K-A-A-Y," raising the pitch of your voice cheerfully. The verbal command always has three words: "Okay, Prince, Come."

COME WHEN CALLED 2. As you say "Okay," simultaneously do two things: Summon the little dog to you by quickly moving your extended right hand to your chest and pull the leash toward you with your left hand. Finish the command, ". . . Prince, Come."

Teaching the hand signal. The verbal command is always accompanied by a hand signal. The hand signal helps eliminate any confusion for the puppy if he is called from a distance and is based on the common gesture that is used to summon a human being from a long way off. The right arm hangs at the side of the body and is raised in a turning, leftward motion as though it were wrapped around a large object.

The entire command for the purposes of this lesson is as follows: "Okay, [Pull the leash with your left hand. Raise your right arm and swing it around to your left side. Complete the gesture and return your arm to its natural position.] . . . Prince, Come." As soon as you have given the hand signal, place your right hand on the leash, using it with the left hand in a hand-over-hand motion to reel the leash in like a fishing line. By the time your puppy reaches you, five feet of leash should be gathered in your hands. Praise the puppy. Practice this procedure at least twelve times.

COME WHEN CALLED 3. *Sits when he reaches you.* The last phase of COME WHEN CALLED is teaching your dog to SIT when he reaches you after obeying the COME command.

Place the puppy in SIT-STAY and walk backward to the end of the leash. Hold the leash high with your left hand, permitting just a little slack, and say, "Okay, Prince, Come." When you say "Okay" give the hand signal with your right hand, but do not pull on the leash. As soon as you have given the hand signal, put your right hand on the leash,  using it in a hand-over-hand motion to reel in the leash, and gather in all but twelve inches as the puppy comes to you.

Holding the remainder of the leash up high with your left hand, command the puppy to SIT as you pull up on the leash, maneuvering him into the SIT position. Praise him lavishly. Repeat this procedure until he gets it right twelve times.

As stated many times before, it is important that your dog associate responding to your call with a happy experience. If you call him to correct him, he will soon stop coming to you. Never call your puppy to you to correct his misbehavior. If you need to correct him, always go to him.

In commanding your puppy to COME, always use the three words specified, "Okay, Prince, Come." *Okay* sets the tone of the command, which is one of pleasant anticipation. It is important that you say it cheerfully. The dog's name is a signal for him to prepare to move forward, while the word *Come* tells him exactly what to do.

Always call your puppy in the same way: "Okay, Prince, Come." Be consistent about this and have the other members of your family do the same.

This completes the puppy training course. Please bear in mind that this course is an *introduction* to obedience training and is appropriate for young dogs and puppies only. A puppy should continue to learn as he grows to maturity. Obedience training should be more demanding and more precise as your puppy grows into an adult dog. There are other training books available that are more appropriate for grown dogs, in addition to training classes, private training sessions from professionals, and clubs focused on competing in obedience trials sponsored by the American Kennel Club, the United Kennel Club, and various others. All of these dog obedience activities are highly useful, interesting, and fun. Happy training and good luck.

PERSONALITY PROFILES OF THE TWENTY-FIVE MOST POPULAR BREEDS

Here, in alphabetical order, are thumbnail profiles of the top twenty-five breeds registered by the American Kennel Club in the year 2000. Of the 1,175,473 purebred dogs registered by AKC that year, 936,996 dogs were in the top twenty-five breeds. These profiles should be very helpful if you are about to buy a puppy and need basic information about the breed you are considering. This information will also be valuable if you already have your dog and are about to begin training.

Basset Hound

A Duffel Bag with Legs

Personality The Basset Hound is one of the great scent-hound breeds developed in France and Belgium centuries ago for the slow-but-precise trailing of small game, such as rabbits. The secret to its success as a great trail dog is its instinct to keep its nose close to the ground as it uses its highly developed sense of smell to find its prey. This has an important influence on its personality. Bassets are slow moving, deliberate, and highly focused once they catch the scent of something interesting.

Basset Hounds are all pleasant dogs, but some are more sensitive than others, while some are very stubborn. Still, they are all fun to hang out with. They are mild-mannered, good-natured dogs. Their faces often look soulful, but their playful behavior will keep you laughing all day long, until you are confronted with their stubborn streak. As amusing as they are, they will test your patience to its limit. They must be obedience trained and given commands in a firm manner.

Mischief Do not be fooled by their barrel-shaped bodies, short legs, and slow movements. Bassets are scent hounds, and these fine hunters can run much faster than you'd think. Although they do not seem very active inside the house, they are strong and can run well when they want to. Do not leave your front door open or you will find yourself chasing your Basset Hound down the street. If you are gone all day, you may get complaints about howling and barking. Digging is one of their great pleasures no matter how unhappy it makes you. As puppies they may be nippy and mouthy. Many Bassets are chewers and can be destructive if you are not alert to this problem. Do not give them access to your possessions until you are certain they will not chew them.

A Word to the Wise Start housebreaking as early as possible. Bassets mature late, so you must be patient throughout their training. Work in a quiet area. Teach the stationary commands, such as SIT, STAY, and DOWN, first. When giving leash corrections be careful not to pinch their long floppy ears with the choke collar. Use a nylon choke collar only. Bassets are sensitive dogs, and you must not jerk too hard when correcting them. Be generous with your praise when they respond properly.

Beagle

Snoopy to the Rescue

Personality The Beagle is a scent hound, a breed that hunts by finding its prey with the sense of smell. The American Kennel Club Standard regards them as miniature Foxhounds. Although they have gentle, loving personalities they are known in the field as courageous dogs with great stamina. Those bred to hunt usually work in a large pack with other Beagles, although some hunt individually.

Beagles are sweet little dogs and do very well with children. But they have high-energy personalities and are very strong willed. They are little dogs with big attitudes, and seem to say, "Why should I have to do this since I'm my own boss?" They have a short attention span, and if you fall under the spell of their good looks and sensitive nature, you will let them get away with murder.

Mischief If it is on the ground, they will pick it up in their mouths. They are four-legged vacuum cleaners. They will get into everything and chew up whatever they can. They also love to dig, so be careful about leaving them alone in the backyard. You could have problems with your neighbors if you do not stop their barking, which is part of their hunting behavior as well as their sense of territory. They will bark at strangers, squirrels, and other small animals if you leave them in the yard alone. They feel compelled to steal food from your table if it is left out and you're not looking. Beagles love to eat. Of course, these things can be corrected with proper training.

A Word to the Wise Beagles are slow learners when it comes to training, so you must be patient. They need lots of praise and motivators, such as favorite toys, as rewards. Because they are

easily distracted, you must train them in a quiet area. Training sessions should be no longer than 10–15 minutes, several times a day. The secret to training Beagles successfully is short sessions that are fun. They need to think training is an enjoyable game. If you pick them up frequently they will always be on your furniture, so it is a good idea to treat them like big dogs and keep them on the floor.

Bichon Frisé

Powder Puff

Personality The Bichon Frisé is a distant relation to the Poodle and a larger version of the Maltese, and they are all descended from water spaniels. The breed originally came from Tenerife, one of the Canary Islands off the coast of Spain, and in essence is a miniaturized water retriever. These double-coated, bundles of white fluff are happy, gentle dogs filled with curiosity and playfulness. They are loving, sociable pets, generally getting along with everyone, including strange dogs. It is impossible to be sad around them, because they are energetic dogs that love to play with adults and children alike and are adorable to look at. They adjust well to small apartments or large houses.

Mischief The number one problem when it comes to Bichon Frisé puppies is housebreaking. Many small dogs take longer to housebreak and then have frequent setbacks for a variety of reasons, including less bladder control or being indulged by permissive owners who fail to meet the terms of housebreaking as described in Chapter Seven, "Housebreaking Your Puppy." Many owners allow them to get away with their mistakes because they are so small and endearing. Bichons enjoy sleeping on your bed and lounging on your furniture unless you stop them. Most behavior problems such as this develop when they

are puppies, because their owners indulge them like babies and
fail to correct them.

A Word to the Wise When housebreaking, you must be consistent. You must stay with the training until it is accomplished,
no matter how long this may take. Determination is the secret to
successfully housebreaking a Bichon Frisé. Obedience training is
a must for this breed, no matter how hard their cuteness makes
it to be firm with them. Use a nylon choke collar, because their
neck is too sensitive for a metal collar. A leather choke collar
is also acceptable for training purposes. Two serious problems
associated with this breed are barking and separation anxiety.
Both problems are often caused by their owners not leaving
them home alone often enough. Obedience training with no dis-
traction is essential. Start training early and be firm in order to
overcome any tendency to coddle them.

Boston Terrier

A Tough-Looking Sweetheart

Personality The Boston Terrier was made in the U.S.A. and
was developed as a cross between the Bulldog and the English
Terrier. If you shake the family tree hard enough, various pit-
fighting breeds will fall out. These are outgoing and extremely
energetic dogs. They have the typical terrier attitude, which
means they are strong willed, stubborn, and single-minded once
they focus on something. They are tough and and do not back
down. Although they are rugged, they are also gentle dogs that
are easy to live with and easy to care for.

Mischief Like most terriers, Bostons love to dig in the ground.
They can be very territorial, and they have a strong prey-drive,

which means that they tend to chase things that cross their paths. Do not let their size fool you, they have big attitudes and stand firm in the face of aggressive behavior from larger dogs. They hold their ground and do not stop.

A Word to the Wise It is very important to socialize Boston Terriers with other dogs at an early age so they get along with them later on. The greatest problem you will have when training them is keeping them focused around distractions. The stationary commands, such as SIT, DOWN, and STAY, will be the most difficult ones to teach. They will learn, but teaching every command will be a bit of a battle because of their terrier attitude. You will need to be patient when training them and not allow yourself to get angry. The best motivator for this breed is praise, although you need to be firm at the appropriate times. The key to successful training is consistency and patience.

Boxer

Serious Face, Sweet Heart

Personality According to the American Kennel Club Standard for the Boxer, this breed is related to almost every type of Bulldog, including the ancient Molossus, which was the root breed of all fighting dogs. But despite their courage and stamina they have been bred to be good-natured, gentle dogs.

Boxers are generally amusing dogs with high-energy personalities. They are strong willed, easily distracted, and some are quite comical. They are typically happy dogs and love to please. It is a fun-loving breed.

Mischief Boxers love to hug people and will inevitably jump all over you. If you give them the opportunity, they will chew your house to shreds. The most difficult training command for them to learn is COME, because they are so easily distracted. They seem to say, "Maybe I will and maybe I won't." The presence of other dogs will command their attention, making it necessary to be firm and demand that they listen to you when you a give a command.

A Word to the Wise When training Boxers, you must constantly hold their attention by giving them lots of praise. Every training command should be taught in the privacy of the home. Once the dog has learned them you may introduce outdoor distractions. If you motivate these dogs with lavish affection, they will respond beautifully. When well trained they become much easier to live with. It is important to be firm and let them know that you're in charge. If you do, they will always respect you, love you, and work to please you.

Bulldog

What a Face!

Personality The original Bulldogs were bred in England for the so-called blood sports of bullbaiting and dogfighting. For that purpose they were selectively bred for toughness and ferocity. These blood sport practices ended in 1835, and since then the breed has been changed radically to be even-tempered, good-natured dogs. The modern Bulldogs' gentle, sweet personality seems to contradict their pushed-in faces with bulging eyes and pointy, protruding lower teeth, reminders of their ancient image as ferocious fighters. In their own inimitable way they are the most adorable dogs on the planet and at times funny, even goofy. Owning a Bulldog now means you will always be amused and have a smile on your face. However, they can be testy. They are also more energetic than you might imagine. Their snoring, wheezing, and gulping for air take a bit of getting used to, and you need a sense of humor when it comes to their eating habits, because food usually drops out of the corners of their mouths as they eat. It is also difficult for them to drink water without it spilling out of their mouths. They are not sloppy. This happens because of the peculiar shape of their jaws.

Mischief As puppies, Bulldogs can be very nippy and mouthy. Destructive chewing will be a serious problem if you do not correct it at an early age. Bulldogs have a strong territorial nature that makes it necessary to socialize them with other people and other dogs as soon as possible. Their territoriality is probably the last vestige of their old fighting days.

A Word to the Wise This breed becomes overheated easily, which makes it necessary to conduct short training sessions, especially in warm weather. We recommend a nylon choke collar for training because of their sensitive necks. Bulldogs are easily distracted, so train them in a quiet area. They tend to mature later than other breeds, which means you must be extra patient in training. Warning: If you feed them from the table, they will be beggars for the rest of their lives.

Chihuahua

A Pocketful of Love

Personality The origins of the Chihuahua are obscure. The breed, however, is identified with Mexico and with slightly larger ancient breeds from Central America, prior to the rise of the Aztecs, circa A.D. 900. Whether they were bred for a specific function or not is unknown. But like most toy breeds, Chihuahuas are endearing pets with personalities that can range from timid to bold, even aggressive, depending on inherited qualities and external influences. Early socialization makes a large difference in this breed's personality. They can be reserved and at times nervous with anyone other than the one owner to whom they have become attached. They are intelligent, alert dogs that are more robust than anyone imagines. Typical Chihuahuas have high-energy personalities and can be rambunctious. They can be self-centered and demanding if they are treated as babies. Because of their very small size, people who love them tend to carry them around in their arms most of the time. This usually leads to shy or aggressive behavior. The only way to ensure a stable personality is to socialize them with other people and other dogs at an early age.

Mischief As with most toy breeds, housebreaking can be difficult, as can preventing them from sleeping on the bed and furniture when you don't want them to. This problem usually occurs because the dog's owner allows him to sleep on the furniture part of the time.

A Word to the Wise When you obedience train these dogs, first teach SIT, STAY, and DOWN, because the leash is less difficult to maneuver with these commands, and this makes training easier. The leash can be awkward when training small dogs and can easily become tangled with execution of commands involving motion, such as HEEL and COME. It is very important that you do not carry these dogs in your arms all the time. Acclimate them to walking on the ground with a leash and collar. Otherwise they will be hard to train, because they are so cute it is hard to stop indulging them. Do not give in. A well-trained dog will make the entire family happier. Do not use a metal choke collar in training. Use a nylon or flat collar of the right size, because of their delicate bodies.

Cocker Spaniel

Long-eared Angels

Personality Cocker Spaniels are land spaniels originally bred in England to assist hunters by finding small game and birds and indicating their location, flushing them on command from their hiding places, and retrieving them once they've been dispatched. Their name derives from the woodcock, a bird they were especially proficient at finding. Like all good hunting dogs, they are very alert, which means they can also be easily distracted. At times you think they are paying attention to you, but they really are concentrating on other sights and sounds around them. Cocker Spaniels are very active, high-energy dogs. At times it is hard to correct them, because they always seem busy, curious, and mischievous. Cockers are sweet, lovable, and huggable puppies that make you wish they would never grow up.

Mischief Housebreaking can be difficult if you do not start the training at an early age. Cocker Spaniels can be excessive wetters owing to their excitable nature. Also, they can often seem to have one doggie mission, which is to chew as many things as they can get their teeth around.

A Word to the Wise Because they are so easily distracted, all training should be done in a quiet area. The stationary commands, such as SIT, STAY, and DOWN-STAY, will be the most difficult to teach successfully because of the breed's high-energy level. The HEEL and COME commands will be easier to teach because these active dogs never want to stop moving.

Dachshund

Little Dog with a Big Attitude

Personality Daschunds are scent hounds and derive from larger hound breeds. In German, the name means *badger dog,* indicating the fact that they have been used in the past as formidable hunters. In various stages of their development in Germany they were used to hunt badger, wild boar, fox, and rabbits. As companion animals they are sweet but strong-willed, high-energy dogs that will run your life if you let them. They're sure to get under your skin, and they just might get under your bedcovers at the same time if you don't let them know who's in charge. These are extremely clever dogs that often outsmart their owners.

Mischief Housebreaking is the primary training difficulty when it comes to Dachshunds. Do not paper train this breed, because it confuses them and encourages inappropriate use of the floor. They love to bark, and if you let them sleep with you in your bed, they will also take naps on all of your furniture. They love to dig and will attempt to do so no matter how much time and money you have spent on your lawn. They can be shy or aggressive if not socialized properly at an early age, with both dogs and people.

A Word to the Wise Make sure housebreaking is your number one priority. Because they are small, lovable dogs, it is easy to allow their housebreaking accidents to go uncorrected. Don't be taken in by their size. Train them as if they were big dogs. Start with stationary commands, such as SIT, STAY, and DOWN, because these commands are easier on their bodies. Dachshunds are vulnerable to developing back problems, and their first training sessions should be as comfortable for them as possible. Be consistent and demanding in the training. Do not be fooled by their adorable nature.

Doberman Pinscher

Black Beauty

Personality Dobies are high-energy dogs, responsive to commands and very alert. They are extremely loyal to their family. Once they are obedience trained they are among the brightest and easiest dogs to handle. They have a high willingness to please and are fine companion animals, even good with children. But socialization with other dogs and other people at a young age is essential if you want your puppy to become a great pet.

There is a misconception that they are antisocial or aggressive, or that they turn on their owners. However, when they are bred properly, socialized, and trained, they are affectionate, obedient, and loyal. According to the American Kennel Club Standard for the Doberman Pinscher, the breed was created from a mixture of shorthaired shepherd dogs, Rottweilers, Black-and-Tan Terriers, and smooth-haired German Pinschers at the turn of the nineteenth century. These are herding breeds, hunting breeds, and breeds that are highly territorial. Combined, they produce a dog that is ideal for guard and protection work as well as making a fine companion animal.

Mischief Because of their energy level, Dobermans will run through your house like a speeding train. They are very athletic and can jump quite high off the ground. If you want to contain them outdoors, make sure your fence is no less than six feet high, though eight feet is better. They are mouthy, especially as puppies, and will use any opportunity they can get to take your hands into their wet mouths. Their territorial nature makes them bark at people and other dogs, sometimes to excess.

A Word to the Wise Start obedience training right away. Dobermans are responsive and learn quickly. However, they are easily distracted and should be trained in a quiet area with no audience. Commands involving movement, such as HEEL and COME, will be the easiest to teach. It is absolutely essential that you socialize this breed right away, with many people and many dogs, in order to make them friendly pets and companions.

German Shepherd

My Hero—The Ultimate Pet and Protector

Personality German Shepherds are strong-willed, high-energy dogs. They are also responsive, alert, sweet and loving to family and friends, and completely loyal. For many they embody true love and devotion and are considered the best pal anyone can have. The key to the Shepherd personality is socialization. If you raise one of these dogs in a loving environment, expose him to a wide variety of adults, children, and other dogs at a young age, you will create an outgoing, friendly, and fun-loving dog. But if you keep the dog confined to the yard, mostly by himself except for his family, chances are you will create a fear-aggressive animal that is not fun to be with. Such a dog will have the opposite of the true German Shepherd personality.

Mischief Shepherds can be very territorial, excessive barkers, and overprotective when they are not properly socialized at an early age. An unsocialized German Shepherd may chase anyone or anything that crosses his path, such as innocent strangers, cats, passing dogs, cars, or anything else in motion, because of the breed's intense prey-drive.

A Word to the Wise Training must start at an early age. An important and highly valuable command to teach is COME WHEN CALLED in order to get control of the dog if he ever gets loose. Getting hit by a car is the leading cause of death in dogs and teaching COME WHEN CALLED is extremely valuable for preventing this. It is very important to understand your dog's personality and adapt your training techniques to it. Dogs of this breed need a job involving responsibility more than most others because of their social attachments, sense of territory, and boundless energy. These dogs were bred to work, which is why they have been so successful as guide dogs, bomb-detection dogs, rescue dogs, narcotic-detection dogs, guard dogs, protection dogs, etc. So when you think of a job for your dog, consider involving him in the sport of agility or obedience trials, flyball, and any of the various dog sports. Bonding with a German Shepherd is the key to gaining control over him, and early obedience training creates the strongest bond possible. All you have to do is reward him extravagantly with love, praise, and affection during training, and your German Shepherd will be a dream dog.

German Shorthaired Pointer

Perpetual Motion

Personality German Shorthaired Pointers are consummate hunting dogs because of their great versatility in the field. In this one breed is combined a pointing bird dog, a keen-nosed night trailer, a proven duck dog, a natural retriever on land and water, as well as an intelligent family watchdog and companion. These highly energetic dogs have a warm, affectionate nature and are very outgoing and friendly. Because they are hunting dogs, they need to run and exercise to work off their built-up energy. They play hard and always seem to be busy. Although they are happy and playful dogs, they occasionally get into trouble in all the wrong places. They can also be stubborn dogs with very strong wills.

Mischief German Shorthaired Pointers are destructive chewers. They will rummage through the garbage and steal food from the table if given the opportunity. Digging is their favorite pastime. Because of their excitable behavior, jumping on people and furniture is also a big problem. They love to play catch-me-if-you-can, so do not leave the front door open!

A Word to the Wise Correct all behavior problems while these dogs are still puppies. Always use a nylon choke collar when obedience training them, because it is not damaging if their long ears become pinched when you pull on the leash or administer a leash correction. A metal choke collar can cut the tip of the ear or cause a hematoma if it causes a hard pinch. These dogs are easily distracted and require a quiet area for training. Emphasize the stationary commands, such as SIT, STAY, and DOWN, in order to gain control as soon as possible over these energetic dogs that will run out the door if given half a chance. Their favorite ball or toy is highly useful as a reward for executing training commands properly. These are referred to as motivators and are effective training tools. Vigorous daily exercise is necessary.

Golden Retriever

Cutest Puppies on the Planet

Personality Golden Retrievers were developed in England, in the early part of the nineteenth century, to assist hunters in the taking of waterfowl and upland game birds. Their job was to locate and retrieve birds that were taken by hunters. They are most useful in the pursuit of wild ducks, geese, and other water-fowl. They will sit absolutely still in a duck blind and dive into the water and swim back with a fallen bird in their mouth, all on command. They are sweet dogs, extremely sensitive, playful, and can always be counted on for enthusiasm-on-demand. However, they can also be strong willed and pushy at times. You have to be careful not to spoil these very lovable but unrelenting dogs by giving in to their every demand. Like clever children, they will exploit those who do not know how to say no. They have big hearts, soulful eyes, and love to be a part of the family.

Mischief Typical Golden Retrievers are even tempered with few if any serious behavior problems. However, they may chew on your possessions, dig up your lawn, or jump on the furniture and all over you as well. If given half a chance, they will steal the food out of your mouth, certainly off the kitchen table. Keep your closets closed because Goldens will grab your shoes, socks, sweaters, or even your underwear when you're not looking. If your Golden doesn't do some or all of these things, then check his papers to be sure he is really a Golden Retriever.

A Word to the Wise Behavior problems must be nipped in the bud before they become serious. Luckily, Goldens are some of the easiest dogs to train. They love to please their owners and will work hard for your praise. Goldens need a job because they love to work. Goldens love to work, whether it's obedience training, participating in the sport of agility or obedience trials. By working them at something you will channel all their energy and give them a sense of well-being. Training them in a quiet area at first makes it easy for them. You can add distractions later to fine-tune the training. Start training at an early age for the best results. Because they are sensitive dogs, do not give them harsh verbal corrections or you will make them shy or submissive and then they become fearful. Goldens are so lovable they can wrap anyone around their paws, so don't fall for their soulful eyes when it's time to train.

Labrador Retriever

A Dog for All Seasons

Personality Labrador Retrievers were originally bred to be strong swimmers in icy water, assisting the fishermen of Newfoundland. By the nineteenth century they had proved to be superb retrievers of waterfowl and became valuable as field dogs. They are high-energy, fun-loving, friendly dogs that are totally devoted to those with whom they live. They are also excitable, strong willed, mischievous, and according to some owners, slapstick comedians. For anyone who wants a dog for all seasons, this is the breed of choice. From the White House to your house, Labs are among the best family pets available.

Mischief Labs love to chew, which can become a serious problem if not corrected early. They also like to *mouth,* which means munching without using their teeth, on whatever is handy, such as newspapers, slippers, and especially your arms and hands. The habit of mouthing can be attributed to the fact that they are retrievers and have been bred to return to hunters with a duck in their mouth. Unfortunately, whatever they mouth becomes drenched with saliva. They will also help themselves to anything they can find, such as a shoe, a towel, or a slice of cake. They will eat anything they can grab off the kitchen counter or dining table. They love to dig up the yard and jump up on people they like, and they usually like everybody.

A Word to the Wise The earlier you train Labs, the better the results you will get. It is best to train them in a private area at first, because they are easily distracted. Training them is a pleasure because they love to please. The more you praise them, the quicker they learn. Motivators, such as balls, toys, or Frisbees, will help the training tremendously when used as a reward. Labs are among the easiest dogs to train.

Maltese

Elegance in White

Personality The Maltese is an ancient dog breed that has always been highly prized by royalty and the aristocracy. They are beautiful to look at and endearing to be with. If the Maltese have a purpose, it is to enrich those with whom they live with companionship and pleasure. These Babes in Toyland are happy, playful, sweet, and delectable dogs. They are impossible to discipline, because they are so cute. All you have to do is pick up a Maltese puppy in your arms and you will just melt. To live with one is like having a prince or princess in your home.

Mischief Housebreaking is the most difficult problem when it comes to the Maltese. Everyone spoils them, and most of their behavior problems are caused by this. They can be noisy, and your neighbors may complain about their barking at anything that comes within a few feet of their front door. When you come home and look for your puppy, check out the furniture. This is where he'll most likely be, since you've most likely allowed him there in the past. Socializing at an early age is necessary to avoid shyness.

A Word to the Wise The biggest mistake you can make is to constantly carry your Maltese around in your arms. This can make the dog insecure when you put him down, or aggressive whenever someone approaches you. It is important to expose this breed to children at a young age, and leash break them while they are still puppies. It is hard for them to believe that they are not the children in the family. Use a nylon choke collar and lightweight leash for training to protect their fragile bodies and delicate fur. Even though they are very small and cute, they still must be trained and taught to be obedient.

Miniature Pinscher

So Delicate–So Tough

Personality Miniature Pinschers (Minpins) are similar in looks to the Doberman Pinscher, but they are more like terriers, especially when it comes to their sense of territory. They love their homes and families and make ideal companion dogs. They are intelligent animals with a feisty temperament. Minpins are spirited, strong-willed, high-energy dogs. They are very alert and stay focused on their owners because they like to please, especially in obedience training. However, they are mischievous, and if you give in to them, they will take advantage of you. Miniature Pinschers are fun to be with and are extremely portable. *Minpins are good to go.*

Mischief The primary problem with this breed is housebreaking. Because they are so territorial, shyness, aggression, and barking can also be major issues if the dogs have not been socialized at an early age with children, adults, and other dogs. They have little tolerance for pulling and roughhousing, so they may not be good for young children. If they are to live with children, they must be raised with a child from puppyhood. Once you allow them on your bed or furniture, they will always be there.

A Word to the Wise Constantly carrying your Miniature Pinscher around in your arms like a baby is a form of pampering that has serious consequences. It tends to create inhibited behavior, possessiveness, and territoriality, which lead to aggressive behavior. It also makes them less sociable with people and other dogs. Minpins should be leash-trained early, always using a lightweight, nylon choke collar and leash because of the dogs' delicate bodies. As you start training, begin with the stationary commands, such as SIT, DOWN, and STAY, because Minpins are so easily distracted. These commands, once taught, make the commands involving movement easier to teach. When training these dogs, always work in a quiet area because they are so easily distracted.

Miniature Schnauzer

Adorable Tough Guy

Personality Developed from the Standard Schnauzer, this German breed is a terrier and was originally a small farm dog, used to hunt vermin. However, their good looks and charming personalities have transformed them into desirable companion animals. Highly intelligent dogs, Miniature Schnauzers are eager to learn, with a strong-willed attitude. They love to work, to please, and enjoy being trained. Although they are stubborn, they are alert and protective. They can charm the pants off any human with their intriguing facial expressions, attentiveness, and desire to play.

Mischief Protect your landscaped grounds, because this breed loves to dig in the grassy dirt. This is a trait of most terriers because of the way they hunt. They follow such prey as rodents or rabbits down into their holes and dig them out. They are very territorial about their homes and the people in their family and will be aggressive. As a result they will bark at everyone and everything that moves close to you or your property unless they are socialized with other dogs and other people at an early age. They can also be destructive chewers.

Word to the Wise Miniature Schnauzers love to work and take to training very well. They learn all the obedience commands easily. When training them it is important to emphasize the DOWN and DOWN-STAY commands. (Because they are so active they tend to move all the time and become easily distracted.) These two commands teach them to remain in place despite the distractions of other dogs, open doors, open gates, or even open car doors. It is a matter of safety. Train them as you would a big dog, even though they are small, because they can be obstinate.

Pomeranian

The Little Lion

Personality Pomeranians are miniaturized "Spitz-type" dogs. Spitz-type dogs are thought to be descended from the sled dogs of Iceland and Lapland. In their larger form, in Europe, they worked as sheep herders. They are big dogs trapped in tiny bodies. They are like balls of fluff and always seem to be smiling and know how to make their owners feel good. They are happy, outgoing, intelligent, and alert. Sometimes they are too alert and full of mischief. They are masters of manipulation and can wrap a dog owner around their paw anytime they want.

Mischief Pomeranians are like jumping beans and love to leap on people when they least expect it. They are always on the furniture, often because that's where the owners encourage them to go. Housebreaking can be a problem, depending on owner tolerance. Pomeranian mischief, such as excessive barking, is allowed to flourish when those who love the dogs the most indulge them the most, which is in almost all cases.

A Word to the Wise Use a small nylon choke collar when obedience training these little dogs. There should be no distractions during training sessions. Be consistent, and demand that they pay attention. Do not indulge their every whim just because they are so cute and small. You will never get them trained that way.

Poodle

Smarter Than People

Personality Poodles originally functioned as water dogs, much like other retrievers, which has an important influence on their personality. Retrievers are not only strong swimmers but intelligent, decision-making dogs. The Poodle personality is sweet, playful, high energy, and extremely responsive but may vary depending on which of the three varieties of the breed you have: Toy, Miniature, or Standard. Toy and Miniature Poodles are both quite jumpy and excitable. They will melt your heart because they are so small and adorable and fit in your arms like a baby. It is difficult to resist carrying them around. Miniatures are a bit larger and not quite as high-strung as the Toy, but nevertheless, energetic and spirited. Both varieties will test your ability to be firm. Standard Poodles are the Ph.D.s of dogdom. They are unusually bright dogs, eager to please, and very responsive to training. Standards are usually more reserved than the smaller varieties, but occasionally one will be edgy. What all three varieties have in common is their keen intelligence and humanlike characteristics.

Mischief The Toy Poodle's biggest problem is housebreaking. Owners tend to baby them too much, which is really a people problem rather than a dog problem. Standard Poodles and Miniature Poodles only have the typical puppy problems (chewing, jumping, nipping, mouthing, pulling, stealing food, etc.), which are easily solved.

A Word to the Wise Poodles excel in obedience training. They are brilliant. You only have to show them what to do, lavish them with praise, and then enjoy the best-trained dog you ever had. All Poodles need a challenge, and athletic competition is perfect for this purpose. If you have a Poodle, consider involving him in agility competition, the sport of flyball, or obedience competition. Since Poodles were originally bred as retrieving dogs, teaching your dog to retrieve will be fun for both of you.

Pug
What Big Eyes You Have

Personality Of Oriental origin, and somewhat similar to the Pekingese, the Pug has always been a companion animal, not surprising given its small size and loving nature. Owning a pug is a satisfying experience because of its outgoing, sweet temperament. However, they are strong-willed dogs and can be stubborn dogs that will not work to please you every time. Nevertheless, they are always warm and cuddly, even tempered and quite charming. They are ideal companions because all they want to do is play and love you. These mighty toys are sturdy, stable, and dignified, and will become your best friend. Pugs are ideal city dogs and apartment dogs because they are so compact and so very social. It's like having a big dog in a small body.

Mischief Like the Energizer Bunny, Pugs are always on the go. They are also easily distracted and somewhat stubborn. It is very easy to spoil them because they are so lovable. It is their lovability that causes owners to tolerate their jumping on people and furniture, as well as their playful nipping and mouthing.

Most people have a hard time correcting these playful charmers, despite their behavior problems.

A Word to the Wise Do not rush the process of obedience training with your Pug. Take all the time you need to teach him each command. Repetition of each command you teach is the way they learn. Be generous with your praise, and consider this an important teaching technique. An abundance of praise will achieve the best training results.

Rottweiler

A Burglar Alarm with a Heart

Personality In all likelihood this breed derived from herding dogs that lived and worked in ancient Rome and were used to drive cattle for the Roman army. Modern Rottweilers were used as police dogs in the early 1900s because they were dependable, rugged, willing workers, with great intelligence and a strong guarding instinct.

These are outgoing, athletic, extremely strong-willed and alert dogs. They are among the best protection dogs in the world, completely loyal and good-natured companions. Their size, weight, and facial expression serve as a visual deterrent to wrongdoers and seem to say to potential aggressors, "Do you feel lucky?" Early socialization is essential so that they are comfortable with other dogs and most people.

Mischief Rottweilers are large, strong dogs that can pull you down the street if they have not been trained to respond to the HEEL command. Obedience training is very important for this breed. They must be taught to respond properly to all the basic commands. In addition to their great strength they are extremely energetic, and if they get too exuberant, they may jump up on you and knock you over. Because of their instinct to chase prey, you must be prepared to maintain strong leash control when dogs, other animals, or passing strangers are close by.

A Word to the Wise HEEL is an essential command for these dogs, considering their large size and great strength. Until they are completely obedience trained, use a metal choke collar and a strong metal leash for the best training results and to maintain complete control. Do not be afraid to use firm corrections. Also vital to their education is the command COME, considering their highly territorial nature and strong prey-chasing drive. The use of lavish praise when training is a great motivator. They thrive on it. It is essential for you to be the "top dog" in the family when living with a Rottweiler.

Shetland Sheepdog

So Smart—So Elegant

Personality There is no doubt that the Shetland Sheepdog, or Sheltie, is, to quote the American Kennel Club, "a working Collie in miniature," which has an important influence on its personality. This diminutive working breed, which can still be used as a herding dog, has evolved into an endearing companion animal because of its desire to please and its sweet, docile nature. Shelties are smart as a whip, and because of their abilities as herding dogs, excel in the competitive sports of Obedience and Agility. They are eager to please, responsive to training, loyal, and affectionate. They can be somewhat sensitive and reserved with strangers. They can also be strong willed.

Mischief Some Shelties are excessive barkers because they are too territorial. Like other herding breeds, they may nip at you from time to time.

A Word to the Wise It is very important to socialize Shelties with other people and dogs at a young age to prevent them from becoming timid or nervous with those not in their family. Obedience training is the key to having a great Shetland Sheepdog. Do not pamper them. If you make obedience training their job, they will love it and so will you.

Shih Tzu

China Doll

Personality Since the beginning of their appearance in documents and paintings, and on objets d'art dating back to the Tang Dynasty (circa A.D. 624), these royal dogs of the Chinese court have served as house pets because of their small size, elegant looks, intelligence, and docile behavior. These are babies that never grow up and never stop playing. Despite their elegant look, they can be uninhibited clowns and are always adorable and sweet, with a princesslike attitude. They seem to say, "Love me, love me, love me, and I'll to anything for you." They are also stubborn at times and will try to run your house if you allow them.

Mischief Difficulty housebreaking is this breed's greatest problem. The only other problem depends on whether or not you think of it as a problem, and that is having them sleep in your bed and on your furniture. If you permit them to sleep with you and sit on the furniture and you like it, then it is not a problem.

A Word to the Wise Since housebreaking is difficult for Shih Tzus, start early. Teach them to walk on a leash even though it is tempting to carry them around in your arms. Shih Tzus must be socialized as soon as possible, with children, other dogs, and adults, otherwise they can get snippy. Begin training indoors with no distractions in order to make it easier on them and yourself. Your cute little baby needs to be trained. Do not neglect to do this. Obedience training makes everyone happy, including the dog.

Siberian Husky

Always Smiling

Personality Siberian Huskies were developed by the Chukchi people of northeastern Asia as moderately fast, high-endurance sled dogs. They are capable of pulling light loads in extremely cold weather for long distances. They are known for their friendliness and nonaggressive temperament. Although they are alert, they are not protective, nor do they function as watchdogs.

Huskies are happy-go-lucky, high-energy dogs most of the time. This is a *feel good* breed and a wonderful family pet. They love to play, especially with children. Because of their boundless energy, they are not for couch potatoes. They are extremely strong willed, but always in a good-natured way. They simply want to do things their own way.

Mischief Siberian Huskies will dig their way back to Siberia if you let them. Those prized flower beds and beautiful bushes—they love them just like you do and will most likely dig them all up and perhaps nibble on them. They love to chew whatever they can find and will gnaw on your best furniture and maybe the baseboards as well.

A Word to the Wise Obedience training is a must if you are going to live happily with a Husky. Channel your puppy's energy into diligent training sessions and practice periods, and he will learn to respond to you beautifully. At first, train your dog in a quiet area, because Huskies become distracted easily. Once your dog has learned several of the commands, you may introduce distractions slowly as you train him. Think of praising your dog for a job well done as a motivator and an important part of the training technique. Generous praise each time your dog does something right creates a happy and well-trained dog. Huskies are more pack oriented than most dogs and need to please. They feel bad if they do not get approval. These are dogs looking for love in all the right places. The more you praise them, the more you motivate them to accept your commands.

Yorkshire Terrier

The Ultimate Four-Legged Baby

Personality Yorkshire Terriers, or Yorkies, originated and developed in Yorkshire, in the north of England, in the nineteenth century. The ideal Yorkie is about seven inches high at the shoulders, and approximately seven pounds in weight. Although they are among the tiniest of dogs, they possess the energized spirit of all terrier breeds and will bravely hunt for small rodents with the best of them. Typically, they get along well with other dogs, and their personalities make them excellent pets. Yorkies are surprisingly feisty dogs, though, considering their very small size, and they are fearless. It's as if Yorkies do not know how small they really are. They are like four-legged prizefighters and will challenge anyone. These mighty mites do not hesitate to talk back, because they think they are the boss, and in many homes that's exactly what they are. However, like so many other toy breeds, they love to be loved. And they are irresistible.

Mischief Difficulty with housebreaking is their biggest problem. To avoid confusion about where the dog must relieve himself, do not paper train him. You must start housebreaking at an early age, or the dog will leave presents for you all over the house, whether it's Christmas or not. Everyone tends to spoil Yorkies and baby them so much that they never get socialized with people outside the family, or other dogs. This often leads to aggressive behavior, which can be a serious problem, even with such small dogs. Because of their territorial nature, they are miniature guard dogs and will bark at strangers. If you allow one to become your sleeping companion, then the entire house becomes his bed.

A Word to the Wise Do not constantly carry these dogs around in your arms as if they were babies. If you do, it will be very hard to get them to walk with you on a leash. Never use a metal collar of any kind, because it damages their fine coats and can be too harsh for their delicate bodies. Use a nylon or flat collar only. Begin obedience training inside your house because Yorkies are easily distracted outdoors. Be consistent. Treat them seriously, like big dogs in little bodies.

INDEX

One of America's most celebrated dog trainers teams up with the premier pet writer in the country to tackle the most common health and behavior problems that dogs experience.

Solutions
0-684-86473-8 • $13.00

The invaluable resource guide to shaping up your lovable canine companion.

The Ultimate Guide to Dog Training
0-684-85646-8 • $12.00